CAPITAL FLIGHT: THE PROBLEM AND POLICY RESPONSES

CAPITAL FLIGHT: THE PROBLEM AND POLICY RESPONSES

Donald R. Lessard and
John Williamson

INSTITUTE FOR INTERNATIONAL ECONOMICS
WASHINGTON, DC
NOVEMBER 1987

Donald R. Lessard was a Visiting Fellow at the Institute and is currently Professor of International Management at the MIT Sloan School of Management. He has published extensively on various aspects of international finance including corporate finance, portfolio investment, and external financing for developing countries.

John Williamson is a Senior Fellow at the Institute for International Economics. He was formerly economics professor at Pontifícia Universade Católica do Rio de Janeiro, University of Warwick, Massachusetts Institute of Technology, University of York, and Princeton University; Advisor to the International Monetary Fund; and Economic Consultant to Her Majesty's Treasury. Williamson has published numerous studies on international monetary issues, including IMF Conditionality, The Failure of World Monetary Reform 1971-74, and Political Economy and International Money.

The authors gratefully acknowledge the many helpful comments of C. Fred Bergsten, José Diaz-Asper, Miguel Rodríguez, and the referees, and the dedicated typing of Debby McGuire.

INSTITUTE FOR INTERNATIONAL ECONOMICS
11 Dupont Circle, NW
Washington, DC 20036
(202) 328-9000 Telex: 248329 CEIP Fax: (202) 328-5432

C. Fred Bergsten, *Director*
Kathleen A. Lynch, *Director of Publications*
Ann L. Beasley, *Production Manager*

The Institute for International Economics was created, and is principally funded, by the German Marshall Fund of the United States.

The views expressed in this publication are those of the authors. This publication is part of the overall program of the Institute, as endorsed by its Board of Directors, but does not necessarily reflect the views of individual members of the Board or the Advisory Committee.

Copyright © 1987 Institute for International Economics. All rights reserved. No part of this book may be reproduced or utilized in any form or by any means, electronic or mechanical, including photocopying, recording, or by information storage or retrieval system, without written permission from the Institute.

Printed in the United States of America 91 90 89 88 87   5 4 3 2 1
Library of Congress Cataloging in Publication Data

Capital Flight

(Policy analyses in international economics; 23)
Papers presented at a conference held October 1986.
Includes References, page 59

 1. Capital movements—Congresses. 2. Capital movements—Developing countries—Congresses. I. Williamson, John, 1937– . II. Lessard, Donald R. III. Institute for International Economics (U.S.) IV. Series.
HG3891.C367 1987   332'.042   87-17279

ISBN 0-88132-059-5

Contents

PREFACE *C. Fred Bergsten* *page ix*

INTRODUCTION *page 1*

1 DEFINITION *page 2*

2 MAGNITUDE *page 5*
   The Balance of Payments Accounts Approach *page 6*
   The Residual Approach *page 6*
   Bank Deposits *page 8*
   Modifications *page 9*
     Inadequacies in Debt Statistics *page 9*
     Trade Credit *page 10*
     Interest Income *page 10*
     Tourism *page 11*
     Misinvoicing *page 11*
     Normal Capital Exports *page 12*
   Preferred Estimates *page 13*
   Other Countries *page 15*
   Time Profile of Outflows *page 16*

3 CAUSES *page 17*
   Empirical Findings *page 23*

4 CONSEQUENCES *page 26*

5 SOURCE-COUNTRY POLICIES *page 31*
Macroeconomic Fundamentals *page 32*
Corruption *page 34*
Domestic Financial Markets *page 35*
Exchange Control *page 37*
Taxation *page 40*

6 HAVEN-COUNTRY POLICIES *page 43*
Taxation *page 45*
Deposit Seeking by Banks *page 47*
World Interest Rates *page 48*

7 CAPITAL REPATRIATION: CABOOSE OR LOCOMOTIVE? *page 49*
What Can Countries Do? *page 51*
Offshore Intermediation *page 53*
Should Countries Seek to Recapture Flight Capital? *page 54*

8 SUMMARY AND CONCLUSIONS *page 55*

REFERENCES *page 59*

APPENDIX

Conference Participants *page 61*

TABLES

1 Schematic balance of payments accounts *page 5*
2 Estimates of resident capital outflow and capital flight, 1976–84 *page 7*
3 Taxonomy of factors explaining international capital flows *page 19*

INSTITUTE FOR INTERNATIONAL ECONOMICS
11 Dupont Circle, NW, Washington, DC 20036
(202) 328–9000   Telex: 248329 CEIP   Fax: (202) 328–5432

C. Fred Bergsten, *Director*

BOARD OF DIRECTORS

Peter G. Peterson, *Chairman*
Anthony M. Solomon
Chairman, Executive Committee

Raymond Barre
W. Michael Blumenthal
Douglas A. Fraser
Alfred Herrhausen
Reginald H. Jones
Frank E. Loy
Donald F. McHenry
Ruben F. Mettler
Saburo Okita
Suliman S. Olayan
I. G. Patel
Karl Otto Pöhl
Edmund T. Pratt, Jr.
David Rockefeller
Donna E. Shalala
Mario Henrique Simonsen
Louis von Planta
Dennis Weatherstone
Marina v.N. Whitman
Andrew Young

Ex officio
C. Fred Bergsten
Richard N. Cooper

Honorary Directors
Alan Greenspan
George P. Shultz

ADVISORY COMMITTEE

Richard N. Cooper, *Chairman*
Robert Baldwin
Lester R. Brown
Rimmer de Vries
Juergen B. Donges
Rudiger Dornbusch
Robert J. Flanagan
Isaiah Frank
Jacob A. Frenkel
Gottfried Haberler
Mahbub ul Haq
Arnold C. Harberger
Dale E. Hathaway
Nurul Islam
Peter B. Kenen
Lawrence R. Klein
Ryutaro Komiya
Lawrence B. Krause
Anne O. Krueger
Paul R. Krugman
Roger M. Kubarych
Robert Z. Lawrence
Assar Lindbeck
Harald B. Malmgren
Rachel McCulloch
Richard R. Nelson
Joseph S. Nye, Jr.
Rudolph A. Oswald
Jacques J. Polak
Jeffrey D. Sachs
Ernest Stern
Philip K. Verleger, Jr.
Henry C. Wallich
Alan Wm. Wolff

Preface

Capital flight has become a topic of major policy concern in the context of Third World debt and development, especially in Latin America. The issue also raises questions about the interaction between economic policies in the industrial and developing countries, and regarding the role of international banks as both lenders to the Third World and depositaries for their capital exports. The Institute thus decided to conduct a comprehensive analysis of the issue, beginning with a conference in October 1986. This study presents the analytical findings and policy recommendations that resulted from that effort.

The Institute has previously conducted a number of studies of the debt problem: *International Debt and the Stability of the World Economy* (1983), *International Debt: Systemic Risk and Policy Response* (1984), and *Mobilizing Bank Lending to Debt Countries* (1987), all by William R. Cline; *Financial Intermediation Beyond the Debt Crisis* (1985) by Donald R. Lessard and John Williamson; and *Bank Lending to Developing Countries: The Policy Alternative* (1985) by C. Fred Bergsten, William R. Cline, and John Williamson. In addition, the overall problems of Latin America were addressed in *Toward Renewed Economic Growth in Latin America* (1986), by Bela Balassa, Gerardo M. Bueno, Pedro-Pablo Kuczynski, and Mario Henrique Simonsen. The present study seeks to extend those earlier analyses by appraising the problem of capital flight and suggesting possible responses to it. The papers prepared for the conference in October 1986 are being published in a companion volume entitled *Capital Flight and Third World Debt*, released simultaneously with this study.

The Institute for International Economics is a private nonprofit research institution for the study and discussion of international economic policy. Its purpose is to analyze important issues in that area, and to develop and communicate practical new approaches for dealing with them. The Institute is completely nonpartisan.

The Institute was created by a generous commitment of funds from the German Marshall Fund of the United States in 1981, and continues to receive substantial support from that source. In addition, major institutional grants are now being received from the Ford Foundation, the William and Flora Hewlett Foundation, and the Alfred P. Sloan Foundation. A number of other foundations and private corporations are contributing to the increasing diversification of the Institute's financial resources.

The Board of Directors bears overall responsibility for the Institute and gives general guidance and approval to its research program—including identification of topics that are likely to become important to international economic policymakers over the medium run (generally, one to three years) and which thus should be addressed by the Institute. The Director, working closely with the staff and outside Advisory Committee, is responsible for the development of particular projects and makes the final decision to publish an individual study.

The Institute hopes that its studies and other activities will contribute to building a stronger foundation for international economic policy around the world. Comments as to how it can best do so are invited from readers of these publications.

C. FRED BERGSTEN
Director
October 1987

Introduction

The subject of capital flight arouses strong emotions. Some observers view it as a symptom of a sick society, a cause of Latin America's failure to recover from the debt problem, and a rational reason for foreign lenders to be leery of increasing their exposure. Others regard the very use of the term "capital flight" as a pejorative description of natural, economically rational responses to the portfolio choices that have confronted wealthy residents of some debtor countries in recent years.

The problem of capital flight is a difficult one because both these views of the issue are essentially correct. It is true that capital flight has been enormously damaging to the economies involved (see "Consequences," below), and that remains true, despite the modest reflow that some countries have experienced recently. In extreme cases it signals a breakdown in social cohesion, with implications that go far beyond its financial impact. But it is also true that it is the result of individual agents' reacting in the way that is posited as rational by economic theory and accepted as normal in industrial countries. This inevitably makes it difficult to resolve the chronic economic problems that the flight of capital has brought in its wake.

This study starts by considering the vexing question of how "capital flight" should be defined; proceeds to assess its magnitude, causes and consequences; and concludes with a discussion of the set of policies that might help to stop and reverse it. The analysis draws extensively (though not exclusively) on a conference that the Institute for International Economics held in October 1986, the proceedings of which are being published simultaneously with this study.

1 Definition

The question has often been posed: why do we refer approvingly to "foreign investment" by Americans, Japanese, and Kuwaitis and use the censorious term "capital flight" to describe the same activity when undertaken by Latin Americans? Is capital flight in fact anything more than capital outflows of which we disapprove, or capital outflows that prove inconvenient to the government of the country losing the money? Must not a distinction between "normal" outflows of capital and "capital flight" be based on the legality of the outflow?

We believe that, as a matter of linguistic principle, terms should be used to mean what normal usage of the English language suggests they mean unless there is overwhelming precedent for a deviant technical usage. At the moment, the uses of the term capital flight are still so varied that there is certainly no overwhelming precedent for any particular usage, deviant or otherwise. Ingo Walter (ch. 5)[1] points out that Webster defines "flight" as "an act or instance of running away." Kindleberger (1937, p. 158) defined capital flight as "abnormal" flows "propelled *from* a country... by... any one or more of a complex list of fears and suspicions." Accordingly, we believe there are both linguistic and economic precedents for defining capital flight as "money that runs away" or "flees." [2]

On this view, one refers to capital flight by Latin Americans but not by Japanese because of a belief that Latin investors are trying to escape the high risks they perceive at home while Japanese investors are responding to what they perceive to be better opportunities abroad. That formulation makes it

---

1. Chapter references are to chapters of the accompanying conference volume, Lessard and Williamson (1987).
2. In another recent study, Michael Deppler and Martin Williamson (1987, p. 41) provided another precedent: "... capital flight may be defined as the acquisition... of a claim on nonresidents that is motivated by the owner's concern that the value of his asset would be subject to discrete losses if his claim continued to be held domestically."

very clear why many economists feel ill-at-ease with such a definition; we take it for granted that both groups of investors will base their decision on a *comparison* of the relative returns and risks involved in investment at home and abroad, and therefore tend to reject any distinction based on picking out just one of those factors. But this is to be excessively purist: it is like refusing to say that a current account deficit is due to overvaluation on the grounds that, at some sufficiently depressed income level, the deficit would vanish. The charge of overvaluation implies some judgment about normal or desirable income levels (for example, "full employment" or "internal balance"). Similarly, a diagnosis of capital flight implies some notion of normal risks and returns abroad, and reflects a judgment that the deviant factor propelling the outflow is the level of domestic risk perceived by some or all residents.

This definition implies that capital flight is not the same as an undesirable capital outflow. Indeed, it is not difficult to think of certain instances of "good" capital flight, such as that involving the French Huguenots in the late seventeenth century or German Jews in the 1930s. In other instances, capital flight may serve the social function of inducing desirable policy changes. Even if the normative perspective is that of the government rather than outside observers such as ourselves, capital flight can surely not be equated with undesirable capital outflow: as Miguel Rodriguez points out (ch. 6), the Venezuelan government actually welcomed the outflow of capital from Venezuela as late as 1981 on the ground that it would help combat inflation. Would we then want to say that there was no capital flight from Venezuela in 1981? And when the Venezuelan government changed its mind about the desirability of that outflow, would it be reclassified as an instance of capital flight after all? Conversely, can we not conceive of instances of capital outflow that the government finds inconvenient that we would not wish to describe as capital flight? Had a Labour government that deplored the British capital outflow of the early 1980s been elected in 1987, would we suddenly have declared Mrs. Thatcher's Britain to have been the victim of capital flight?

Our concept of flight capital as that which flees from the perception of abnormal risks at home implies that the question of the legality of the outflow is distinct from that of whether it is "normal" or "fleeing." As it happens, there were no exchange controls making the export of capital illegal when what are usually considered the major episodes of capital flight took place from Argentina, Mexico, and Venezuela. What our definition does suggest is that measurement of capital flight requires an attempt to measure the outflow of capital that may be considered "normal" and deduct this from the total outflow.

Dooley (1986) has made an explicit attempt to distinguish between capital outflows "motivated by normal portfolio decisions" and those "based on the desire to place assets beyond the control of domestic authorities." His technique, which involves taking as normal those outflows that generate a stream of income recorded in the balance of payments statistics, is subject to challenge (see "Magnitudes," below); but his concept of abnormal outflows as those motivated by an attempt to escape the control of the domestic authorities seems much the same as our concept of those fleeing abnormal risks at home.

Some participants in the conference, such as Miguel Rodriguez, would argue that the "normal" capital outflow from a capital-short developing country should be zero. To paraphrase Tobin (1977), "It takes a heap of Harberger triangles to fill a foreign exchange gap." Presumably, exceptions might be made for foreign investments that bring exceptionally high returns to the domestic economy, typically because of a benefit over and above the yield to the investor—such as direct investment that creates a demand for additional exports or assures a supply of raw materials, export credits that secure additional export orders, or bank claims that act as collateral to secure additional credits. But this is to revert to a normative definition, in which capital flight is defined to be that part of the outflow of capital owned by domestic residents that is by some criterion disadvantageous to the national economy.

In the end, we decided not to concentrate on measuring "normal outflows," or therefore "capital flight," but rather "resident capital outflow." We indeed argue below (see "Consequences") that the loss of savings and financial intermediation to the domestic economy resulting from resident capital outflow normally brings some loss to the national economy (and indeed to the world economy), except when it brings abnormally high returns, as instanced above, whether the outflow is normal portfolio diversification or abnormal flight. This is a good reason for concentrating on measuring resident capital outflow. As long as normal outflows for portfolio diversification remain small, the economic cost imposed by resident capital outflow will be modest. When normal outflows are reinforced by money fleeing abnormal risks, the cost will escalate. This is about as good a reason as seems to exist for continuing to use the emotive term capital flight to describe such episodes.

TABLE 1 **Schematic balance of payments accounts**

Exports of goods and nonfactor services	A
Imports of goods and nonfactor services	B
Investment income	C
Debt-service payments	D
Net remittances and transfers	E
Total current account balance $(A - B + C - D + E)$	F
Direct investment	G
Foreign loans, minus amortization	H
Increase in foreign assets of domestic banking system	I
Resident capital outflow: into long-term assets	J
Resident capital outflow: into short-term assets	K
Total capital account balance $(G + H - I - J - K)$	L
Errors and omissions $(N - F - L)$	M
Increase in reserves	N

2 Magnitude

The discussion in this section will be illustrated by table 1, which shows a stylized set of balance of payments accounts. We are aiming to estimate resident capital outflow, items J and K in table 1, without much emphasis on identifying some part of the flow as "normal" and therefore deducting it to get a figure for capital flight. (It has sometimes been assumed that flows into long-term assets, J, are more likely to involve normal portfolio diversification, while those into short-term assets, K, are likely to involve flight capital.)

The basic reason that it is difficult to measure the size of capital flight, apart from the ambiguity of the concept, is that investors fleeing the perception of abnormal risks at home are unlikely to make a point of informing the compilers of balance of payments statistics of their actions. This means that item K, in particular, is usually very poorly measured.

In an attempt to circumvent this difficulty, three conceptually distinct approaches to the measurement of capital flight have been developed in the recent literature.

We start this section by describing these three approaches, proceed to examine a number of modifications that have been proposed, and conclude by looking at what is implied for estimates of resident capital outflow.

The Balance of Payments Accounts Approach

The obvious and traditional approach to measurement involves drawing on the balance of payments accounts. There has been a longstanding presumption that errors and omissions arise primarily because of a failure to measure many movements of private short-term capital, and therefore that it is appropriate to add them (M) to the recorded flows of short-term capital (K) in order to get an estimate of total flows. This approach was adopted by Cuddington (1986) and Dooley et al. (1986) in two of the pioneering studies of capital flight.

Table 2, row 1, shows estimates of the cumulative outflow of resident capital from six debtor countries over the period 1976–84 using this measurement technique. The definition used is that of Cuddington (1986), while the actual numbers come from the Cumby-Levich consistent data set (ch. 3).

The Residual Approach

Apparently spurred by a feeling that the relevant items in the balance of payments accounts were extremely tenuous, several recent analyses have broken away from this traditional approach to estimate capital outflow as a residual. The studies of the World Bank (1985), Erbe (1985), and Morgan Guaranty (1986) took the increase in a country's recorded external debt over a period, added the inflow of capital on account of direct investment (G), and subtracted the current account deficit (F) plus the increase in official reserves (N), and in some cases other elements, notably the increase in foreign lending by domestic banks (I). The logic of this was presumably that the recorded increase in foreign debt gave a better measure of net new foreign loans than the figure (H) in the balance of payments accounts, since otherwise this is just an indirect method of calculating $J + K + M$.

It turns out that, when measured on a consistent data set, resident capital outflow measured in this second way is almost invariably substantially greater

TABLE 2   **Estimates of resident capital outflow and capital flight, 1976–84**
(billion dollars)

	Argentina	Brazil	Korea	Mexico	Philippines	Venezuela	Total
1. Cuddington measure	16.0	−0.1	2.8	36.2	3.7	13.1	71.7
2. Morgan Guaranty measure	25.0	17.3	3.5	53.4	3.7	29.6	132.5
3. Bank deposits (end-1984)	8.2	8.8	0.4	15.1	1.0	12.2	45.7
4. Interest-compounding adjustment	4.9	0.0	n.a.	17.2[a]	n.a.	1.9	n.a.
5. Misinvoicing adjustment	−5.4	−2.1	−10.8	−18.4	n.a.	0.0	−36.7
6. Stock of "legitimate" resident external capital, end-1984	2.4	12.0	6.5	18.9	4.8	2.5	37.1
7. Zedillo's residual	n.a.	n.a.	n.a.	26.0	n.a.	n.a.	n.a.
8. Preferred measure	16	9	0	27	4	30	86

n.a. not available.
Source: Row 1, Cumby-Levich (ch. 3) estimate of Cuddington measure using consistent data set. Row 2, Cumby-Levich (ch. 3) estimate of Morgan-Guaranty measure using consistent data set. Row 3, *International Financial Statistics*. Row 4, Cuddington (ch. 3, table 3.2). Row 5, Gulati (ch. 3). Row 6, Cumby-Levich (ch. 3) estimate of Dooley measure. Row 7, Zedillo (ch. 7). Row 8, see text.
a. This estimate is an exaggeration inasmuch as the Mexican balance of payments figures already contain some allowance.

than that measured in the first way (compare the first two rows of table 2 and also Cumby and Levich, ch. 3, tables 1–6 for annual comparisons). For example, Cuddington's measure of private resident capital outflow from Mexico over the period 1976–84 is $36.2 billion, as against $53.4 billion on Morgan Guaranty's measure; for all six countries for which figures were compiled from a consistent data set by Cumby and Levich, the difference was $71.7 billion versus $132.5 billion (table 2). These differences are far too large to be accounted for by *long-term* resident capital outflow (J), which is the only conceptual difference that would lead to a larger figure being yielded by the residual measure. It follows that at least one of these two measures must be subject to large and persistent measurement error: we discuss below which of the two is most at fault.

Bank Deposits

A third approach involves measurement of the increase in recorded foreign bank deposits owned by a country's residents. It is of course necessary to use a statistical source that distinguishes private from official holdings, which the older statistical series, those of the Bank for International Settlements (BIS), do not, but which the new series of the International Monetary Fund (IMF) do. The third row of table 2 shows the IMF figures for the stock of private bank deposits held abroad at the end of 1984.[3] In every case except that of Brazil, the recorded level of bank deposits is smaller than the estimates of cumulative resident capital outflow derived from either of the first two sources, even though presumably some of the bank deposits originate from prior to 1976.

This is not a surprise, since by no means all private funds held abroad get recorded in IMF statistics, for three reasons: some funds are held in bank deposits outside the major (reporting) financial centers; the nationality of the depositor is not always known or reported accurately; and substantial funds are held in assets other than bank deposits. Because the statistics for bank deposits underestimate the sums held abroad, the increase in those deposits will be an inaccurate (typically low) measure of capital outflow. This source can nevertheless be useful for certain purposes, for example, in forming an

---

3. Because the IMF data series commence only in 1981, it is not possible to show the increase in bank deposits over the period 1976–84 to provide symmetry with the previous two measures.

estimate of the minimum sum being held in liquid form abroad and therefore potentially available for repatriation (for which purpose those data are indeed used by Arellano and Ramos, ch. 7).

Modifications

Several of the papers presented to the Institute's conference on capital flight, and discussion provoked by those papers, led us to conclude that none of the three measures of resident capital outflow presented above can be considered at all satisfactory. We proceed to describe and assess the several criticisms that came to light and, where possible, to suggest the modifications in the statistics that they call for.

INADEQUACIES IN DEBT STATISTICS

Zedillo (ch. 7) argues forcefully that, at least in the case of Mexico, the statistics used by Morgan Guaranty and others to estimate changes in external debt are egregiously misleading. The biggest problem, which appears to apply to some other countries as well, is that the coverage of debt statistics has improved markedly since 1982. Prior to the debt crisis, there was neither a legal requirement nor any motivation for the registration of Mexican private-sector external debt, and in consequence very little was registered. Since then, the statistical coverage has become much more complete, so that the recorded debt increased markedly in 1983–84 despite a modest level of actual new foreign borrowing. This leads to exaggerated estimates of capital flight over that period, although it suggests also that actual capital flight was larger in earlier years when debt accumulation was being underestimated. Incredible as it may seem, this elementary but important point has not been noted by the World Bank, which compiles the debt figures and used them to estimate capital flight (World Bank 1985, p. 64), or by other users such as Morgan Guaranty.

A second problem arises from exchange rate changes. When the dollar depreciates (appreciates), the dollar value of debt denominated in nondollar currencies increases (decreases), without any new borrowing taking place. This factor tended to depress the recorded increase in debt, and thus decrease estimates of capital flight, over the period from 1980 to February 1985, and has subsequently tended to exaggerate estimates. It is not a major factor in Mexico, where over 90 percent of the debt is dollar-denominated, but may be more significant elsewhere.[4]

TRADE CREDIT

Ernesto Zedillo (ch.7) also points out that Mexico suffered a major loss of trade credit after 1982, including a decline in suppliers' credits, on account of both the fall in imports and a reduction in the willingness of foreigners to extend such credits. He argues that estimates of this effect were available in the Mexican balance of payments statistics and should have been introduced in constructing estimates of capital flight.

INTEREST INCOME

Ernesto Zedillo, and also William R. Cline (ch. 3, discussion), argue that interest income earned on bank deposits (and other assets) already held abroad should not be counted as a part of capital flight. The Mexican authorities in fact estimate such interest earnings and include them as a credit in the current account statistics even though the money never enters the country. This reduces the current account deficit that is subtracted from the increase in foreign debt under the residual approach to estimating private resident capital outflow, and increases the "errors and omissions" item under the balance of payments accounts approach, in both cases increasing measured capital flight.

If the objective is to measure capital that is fleeing the country, a case can be made for arguing that, since this money was never in the country, it can hardly flee. But since we wish to measure resident capital outflow rather than capital flight, reinvested interest earnings can reasonably be included as a part of the outflow in view of the customary balance of payments accounting convention of including imputed foreign income as a credit item. Thus, we wish to include it in the measure on which we focus. As noted above, Mexico includes imputed interest on identified claims held abroad by Mexicans (and

---

4. See Cumby and Levich (ch. 3) for illustrative calculations of the importance of this factor.

not just interest recorded as paid to Mexicans), but other countries do not make such estimates. Cuddington (ch. 4) has made estimates of imputed interest income for three of the countries shown in table 2; his estimates are presented in row 4.

TOURISM

Cline also argues that, in the Mexican case, income from tourism and border transactions should be excluded from current account earnings, and therefore should not be included in capital flight even when Mexican residents use these earnings to increase their foreign bank deposits. His argument is that both tourist earnings and income from border transactions are traded in the free rather than the official market, and are therefore not available to the government (unless the authorities enter the free market as a buyer of dollars). He argues that it is misleading to treat earnings in the free market on a par with those in the official market when estimating the likelihood that future borrowing will seep out through capital flight by relating past flight to past borrowing. It is easy to agree with the last contention, which deals with the availability of cash flow for debt service, while still finding it natural to include all earnings used to increase Mexican private foreign assets as a part of capital flight. And resident capital outflow most certainly includes deposits financed by earnings on the free market.

MISINVOICING

As explained in depth by Gulati (ch. 3), capital flight can be effected by underinvoicing exports or overinvoicing imports. In the first case, exporters are not required to surrender to the authorities the full dollar value of their export receipts, and hence can build up holdings of foreign exchange. In the second case, importers receive more foreign exchange than they need to pay their foreign suppliers and can again use the balance to add to their foreign assets. In neither case is the extent of such operations detectable from the statistics, except those on foreign bank deposits, discussed up to now: errors and omissions (M in table 1) is not swelled when A falls or B rises to finance something that is not recorded under K.

In its influential article, Morgan Guaranty (1986) cited a number of cases where there was prima facie evidence that trade misinvoicing had been an important conduit of capital flight. The article implied that there was a presumption that capital flight was in general being underestimated by the failure to add in the effect of trade misinvoicing. It seems that Morgan Guaranty was wrong. In his detailed study in chapter 3, Gulati's systematic comparison of the bilateral trade data of nine debtor countries—Argentina, Brazil, Chile, Korea, Mexico, Peru, Philippines, Uruguay, and Venezuela— with the corresponding measures of the same trade flows by the industrial countries, finds that the underinvoicing of exports (which did occur in a majority of countries)[5] was in most cases outweighed by underinvoicing of imports. The motive was presumably to reduce customs charges or to circumvent import controls designed to limit the permissible value of imports. When an importer underinvoices imports for such motives, he does not qualify for official foreign exchange to cover the full value of his purchases, and hence has to draw down his foreign exchange holdings (or else buy foreign exchange on the parallel market, which means that someone else has to draw on their holdings). The current account deficit is underestimated and the resident capital outflow is overestimated. According to Gulati's estimates, these effects are large for some countries, especially Mexico, Korea and Argentina (see table 2, row 5).

NORMAL CAPITAL EXPORTS

It was argued in the discussion on definitions that the concept of flight capital as that which flees demands that a deduction for the "normal" export of capital should be made from total resident capital outflow in order to end up with a measure of "capital flight." Such an adjustment has been proposed by Dooley (1986), based on the assumption that "normal" capital outflow can be identified with that which subsequently generates an interest return to the capital-exporting country identified in the balance of payments statistics. He suggests taking the recorded interest income of each debtor country and

---

5. However, Guzman and Alvarez (1987) show that, in the case of Mexico, the apparent underinvoicing of exports found by Gulati seems to be completely explicable by a series of adjustments in the Mexican figures, for example, to include the gross value of sales by the "in bond" assembly industries rather than just the Mexican value-added. Unless similar factors operate on the import side, this implies that the usual estimates of Mexican capital flight are even more exaggerated than Gulati claims.

calculating the outstanding stock of foreign capital that would have been needed to generate that interest flow for each debtor country, given prevailing international interest rates. The Cumby-Levich estimates of this stock are shown in table 2, row 6.

It is not always true, however, that balance of payments figures are built up from transactions reported by those involved. For example, interest receipts in the US payments accounts are estimated on the basis of figures for various types of capital stock and the associated interest rates, rather than reports from recipients of interest. Similarly, the Mexican statisticians include in investment income an allowance for the imputed interest on foreign assets even when no income is remitted. In such instances, Dooley's method will underestimate the volume of capital that does not generate returns to the domestic economy. Another problem with his approach is that outflows that do not generate financial returns (such as investment in real estate for vacation homes) are ipso facto classified as flight capital.

Preferred Estimates

We are now in a position to express some views about the construction of preferred estimates of resident capital outflows.

First, since we believe it is more relevant to measure outflow than flight per se, we do not make any deduction on account of "normal" capital outflows.

Second, we treat the estimates of bank deposits in table 2, row 3, as minimum estimates of cumulative resident capital outflow, and ignore them when a preferred source yields a higher figure.

Third, we note Zedillo's estimate of the residual Mexican capital outflow, after adjusting for the increase in the coverage of registered debt, the rundown in trade credit extended to Mexico, and after deducting imputed interest on bank deposits held abroad by Mexicans. We regard the first two adjustments, but not the third, as appropriate from our perspective. The estimate of the interest-compounding (i.e., third) adjustment in table 2, row 4, is $17.2 billion; adding this to Zedillo's figure would give $43.2 billion. However, this is an overestimate inasmuch as the interest-compounding adjustment does not recognize that the Mexican balance of payments figures already make an allowance for interest income. The figure based on Cuddington's approach may therefore be the right order of magnitude.

Fourth, we have to take account of Gulati's estimates of the impact of misinvoicing. This is an effect that in principle should be added to any of the other estimates (apart from bank deposits), but in several cases its addition would lead to implausibly low estimates. We therefore treat it case by case, as discussed below.

For Argentina, it is known that there was substantial underinvoicing of imports, especially armaments, and we therefore deduct Gulati's estimate from the Cuddington measure, and add the interest-compounding adjustment, to get a preferred estimate of resident capital outflow of about $16 billion over the period 1976–84.

For Brazil, Cuddington's measure, even without Gulati's correction, gives a net inflow. This is not plausible in view of the size of external bank deposits owned by Brazilians. We therefore round up the latter to get $9 billion as our preferred measure.

Gulati's estimate of the misinvoicing adjustment for Korea dwarfs both estimates of resident capital outflow. Unlike most other countries, however, Korea shows large and persistent overinvoicing of exports. The only plausible explanation for this seems to be an attempt to qualify for large export subsidies, or possibly to establish property rights in anticipated future "voluntary export restraints." But it is scarcely conceivable that Korean firms actually draw on foreign bank deposits (which anyway they do not have, see table 2, row 3) in order to buy local currency equal to the value of the declared invoices. Thus, a good part of Gulati's misinvoicing figure is probably illusory. We assume that resident capital outflow was zero.

Gulati again has a very high estimate of the overestimation of capital outflow in the Mexican case. If that figure is deducted from Cuddington's measure, it leads to an estimate of capital outflow scarcely greater than the stock of identified Mexican-owned foreign bank deposits. We therefore deduct half of the misinvoicing estimate from Cuddington's figure, ending up with a figure close to Zedillo's.

The Philippines is easy: there is no estimate of misinvoicing, and no disagreement between the first two measures. (This does not, unfortunately, guarantee that $4 billion is the right figure!)

Gulati's estimate for Venezuela showed no net impact of misinvoicing. But in this case Cuddington's measure is hardly larger than the stock of Venezuelan-owned bank deposits, and this seems implausibly small. Indeed, in the Venezuelan case the capital inflows recorded in the balance of payments statistics are known to have been underestimated up to 1983, so that the Morgan Guaranty figure is preferable.

Clearly the above procedures are ad hoc. They reflect the considerable uncertainty that still surrounds the estimation of resident capital outflows. Nevertheless, we do believe that some facts are reasonably certain:

- that the scale of resident capital outflows has been very substantial in relation to, for example, the size of foreign debt
- that the scale of such outflows has, however, been exaggerated by some statistical methods, notably that adopted, inter alia, by Morgan Guaranty
- that the three principal countries involved are Argentina, Mexico, and Venezuela.

Other Countries

Besides the six countries analyzed at length, above, a number of others have been mentioned in one place or another (for example, Erbe 1985, Morgan Guaranty 1986) as having suffered significant capital flight at some time in the last few years. Unfortunately, there is in most cases no quantification of the scale of resident capital outflow that we consider to be at all reliable, and hence we merely list the countries we have seen mentioned:

Bolivia	Jordan
Cameroon	Malaysia
Chile	Nigeria
Colombia	Peru
Costa Rica	South Africa
Ecuador	Syria
Egypt	Tunisia
El Salvador	Turkey
Guatemala	Uruguay
India	Zambia
Indonesia	Zaire
Jamaica	

However, a recent study by Deppler and Williamson (1987) estimated both capital outflows and capital flight over the period 1975–85 for the aggregate of capital-importing developing countries. Of five different concepts that they measure, the one closest to our concept of resident capital outflow is what they call the "narrow measure of capital outflows." This is put at $153 billion from the end of 1974 to the end of 1985. This may be compared with our estimate of an outflow of $86 billion over 1976-84 from six countries that collectively have about 25 percent of the exports, 30 percent of the GDP and 50 percent of the bank loans of all capital-importing developing countries.

Time Profile of Outflows

Certain facts also seem to be fairly unambiguous about the time path of resident capital outflows from the major capital-flight countries (for details, see the lower part of the appendix tables in Cumby and Levich, ch. 3).

For Argentina, the outflow lasted from 1978–83, with a peak in 1981, and was followed by some repatriation. According to Morgan Guaranty (1987), this has totaled over $2 billion. However, newspaper reports as this goes to press speak of a renewed outflow following the Peronist election gains (September 1987).

In Brazil, the outflow was much more irregular, with most sources estimating some reflow in 1981. However, the outflow seems to have resumed afterwards and to be still continuing.

In the case of Mexico, the initial flight of 1973–77 peaked in 1976, was followed by a respite or even modest repatriation in the late 1970s, until the truly massive outflow of the early 1980s got under way around 1980 (the precise date differs between one source and another, from 1979 to 1981). The outflow eased after its peak in the first half of 1982, but estimates differ drastically by how much; Zedillo's estimate that it declined to a relatively modest level in 1984–85 appears plausible. There was a sizable reflow in 1986, estimated by Guzman and Alvarez (1987) to have amounted to $1.2 billion. This seems to have increased further in 1987, reportedly to over $2 billion in the first five months of the year.

In Venezuela, major capital flight got under way in 1979 and an outflow has continued to the present day. The period of massive outflows was from 1981 until February 1983.

The estimates of Deppler and Williamson (1987) for all capital-importing developing countries confirm the picture of peak outflows—at an annual rate of over $22 billion—in 1979–82. In 1975–78 they estimate that outflows averaged almost $7 billion per year, while in 1983–85 they were just over $9 billion per year. Morgan Guaranty (1987) estimates that for 10 countries (our six except Korea, plus Chile, Colombia, Ecuador, Nigeria, and Peru) the outflow declined from almost $19 billion in 1983 to $8 billion in 1984, $5 billion in 1985, and changed sign to a reflow of almost $2 billion in 1986.

3 Causes

At the most general level, resident capital outflow results from a difference in perceived, risk-adjusted returns in source and haven countries. Most discussion and research has focused on source-country circumstances, which is hardly surprising since the very concept of capital flight is "that which flees." In view of our own interest in resident capital outflow rather than capital flight per se, we investigate causes in the rest of the world as well as in source countries. In fact, however, we see little reason to doubt that major capital outflows are associated primarily with source-country policies: episodes of capital flight in various countries have not coincided closely.[6]

Even if one concentrates on the source-country side of the equation, many factors help explain international capital flows. These factors may operate at two different levels. Factors such as natural resource discoveries, changes in terms of trade or technologies that alter the value of national endowments, effective industrial policies, or demographic shifts may cause the economic return on capital in a particular country to tend to diverge from the world level.

In addition to these "fundamental" factors, national macroeconomic and regulatory policies may cause the financial return—the return realized by a private investor—to diverge from the underlying economic returns to a greater extent than in the world economy at large.[7] Higher tax rates will cause such a divergence. So does financial repression—ceilings on deposit rates, required reserves that bear less than the market rate of interest, and directed investment or lending at less than market rates. Price controls and bureaucratic restrictions can also drive a wedge between economic and financial returns.

While all these factors affect expected financial returns and risks—the determinants of private capital flows—some of them have different impacts

---

6. The average of the rank order correlation of episodes in terms of severity among Argentina, Mexico, and Venezuela is 0.57; adding Brazil reduces the coefficient to 0.22; adding Korea and the Philippines as well reduces the coefficient to only 0.11.

7. We use the terms economic and financial returns in the way they are normally defined in the public finance and development literatures. Economic returns (and risks) refer to the total returns to the society of a particular activity, adjusted for price distortions and externalities. Financial returns refer to total returns to private investors, calculated at market prices, net of explicit and implicit taxes. (These concepts have sometimes been described by the terms "social" and "private" returns respectively.)

on the risk-adjusted financial returns to certain classes of investors, particularly residents versus nonresidents. There are two reasons for this. First, many taxes, constraints, and other political or fiscal risks do not apply equally to all investors. Second, some investors have a comparative advantage in bearing particular risks because of differing risk preferences, abilities to diversify the risks in question, and abilities to mitigate these risks. If nonresidents are less exposed to the risk of their claims' losing value in the event of a financial crisis (because, for example, they are denominated in foreign exchange), an increase in the likelihood of such a crisis will cause nonresident capital to replace resident capital. Similarly, if interest-rate ceilings apply to resident deposits, but not to loans from nonresidents, foreign funds will replace resident deposits, effectively arbitraging the interest ceiling.

Table 3 presents a taxonomy of various factors that give rise to international capital flows. The upper left quadrant identifies those factors that explain "normal" one-way, aggregate capital movements on the basis of differences in (risk-adjusted) economic returns across countries. These are the factors that give rise to a balance of investment opportunities relative to investible resources that is out of step with the world, the classic determinants of international capital flows that are typically viewed as being reflected in differences in real interest rates.[8] The upper right quadrant includes those additional factors that give rise to two-way flows—"normal" portfolio diversification—again on the basis of economic returns. These include differences in risk preferences and the ability to diversify particular risks across, as opposed to within, national boundaries.[9] The lower left quadrant captures government interventions that create wedges between economic and financial risk-adjusted returns, and give rise to one-way capital flows *incremental* to those that would take place on the basis of the underlying economic returns. The lower right quadrant identifies those interventions that cause two-way, round-trip capital flows, again incremental to those that would take place on the basis of the underlying economic risks and returns.

Most theoretical and empirical studies of capital flight have interpreted it as that subset of capital outflows that are propelled by source-country policies

---

8. Of course, in a frictionless capital market, differences in interest rates would never materialize since capital flows would serve to equate them. Further, actual observed differences in rates often reflect the types of barriers and distortions captured in the lower two quadrants.

9. For a discussion of these risk-return factors in determining international capital flows, see Williamson (1983, section 9.3).

TABLE 3 **Taxonomy of factors explaining international capital flows**

	One-way flows	Two-way flows
Economic risks and returns	Natural resource endowments Terms of trade Technological changes Demographic shifts General economic management	Differences in absolute riskiness of economies Low correlation of risky outcomes across countries Differences in investor risk preferences
Financial risk and returns, relative to economic	Taxes (deviations from world levels) Inflation Default on government obligations Devaluation Financial repression Taxes on financial intermediation Political instability, potential confiscation	Differences in taxes and their incidence between residents and nonresidents Differences in nature and incidence of country risk Asymmetric application of guarantees Different interest ceilings for residents and nonresidents Different access to foreign-exchange denominated claims.

and that are, somehow, abnormal. Therefore, they have typically emphasized those factors that drive a wedge between economic and financial returns, whether they operate across the board or asymmetrically among residents and nonresidents—those captured in the lower half of table 3. Some studies have also included a subset of those factors that explain differences in aggregate economic returns as well, on the premise that "underlying" and "policy-based" factors can never be completely separated.

Given the complexity of the phenomenon, most studies take partial perspectives that fall into one of two groups. Some economists, including Cuddington (1986 and ch. 4), Conesa (1987), and Dornbusch (1985), focus on the *overall investment climate,* stressing those factors like overvaluation, fiscal deficits, and inflation that influence the financial attractiveness of source-country assets relative to the world standard regardless of who holds them, and thus explain one-way private flows—those included in the left half of table 3. Others, including Dooley (1986 and discussion, ch. 3), Khan and Ul Haque (1985), Eaton (1987), and Ize and Ortiz (1987), point to *discriminatory treatment* of resident capital in the form of differential taxation, financial repression, different currency of denomination, or investment guarantees and their subordination to nonresident claims in the event of financial crisis, and thus explain resident capital outflows that coincide with nonresident inflows. Each approach can be relevant in a particular context.

Much of the accumulation of foreign assets by the domestic private sector in Latin America in recent years has coincided with external borrowing by the sovereign. Thus, the pattern of net capital flows has been much different, typically smaller and often of the opposite sign, than that of resident capital flows. The investment climate approach does not explain this phenomenon of capital simultaneously leaving and entering the country. The discriminatory treatment approach, though, does provide an answer: resident claims are in effect subordinated to foreign claims since these involve a contractual obligation subject to commercial sanctions, which the claims of residents do not. Eaton (1987), for example, stresses the fact that, by explicitly or implicitly guaranteeing external but not internal borrowings, governments create a differential between expected returns to domestic and foreign claimants, generating round-trip flows.

A critical element in both perspectives is that capital flight is typically a reaction to risks associated with domestic assets rather than merely differences in promised rates of interest or return in the two markets. Quoted interest rates in the source country, in fact, may be higher than those elsewhere, but the set of investments offering expected, risk-adjusted returns that match the world standard may be limited or nonexistent.

The risks to which domestic assets are exposed include, among others, inflation, devaluation in excess of the anticipations reflected in domestic interest rates, limits on convertibility of local claims, confiscatory taxation or even confiscation. All are "country risks" in that they involve some element of policy choice on the part of the sovereign.[10] While country risk

---

10. For a definitive review of the theory of country risk as it applies to sovereign borrowing, see Eaton, Gersovitz, and Stiglitz (1986). Lessard (1987) discusses its implications for a wider set of claims.

is typically associated with claims against a country held by outsiders, for example, commercial banks, it also extends to domestic holders of money or other financial assets. In fact, in many cases it is more severe for these claims than for the outside claims. The critical characteristic of such risks is that they derive at least in part from the possibility of sovereign acts in response to circumstances under which either the ability or willingness of the sovereign to meet its total commitments is impaired.

While there is no question that country risk in the form of actual or threatened default is a major risk to lenders to developing countries, the response of these governments to financial crises often generates risks of even greater magnitude to resident asset holders. Consider the "Mexican rescue" of 1982.[11] In the process of stepping back from the brink of default on its external obligations, Mexico underwent a major spiral of devaluation and inflation which almost totally wiped out the value of obligations denominated in Mexican pesos, assets that were held predominantly by Mexican residents. It also imposed exchange controls, effectively halving the value of obligations such as Mex-dollar deposits and petrobonds that were denominated in dollars but payable only within Mexico. These claims, too, were predominantly held by Mexican investors. Finally, it imposed drastic austerity measures coupled with radical structural changes on the domestic economy, again reducing the value of many existing businesses and the direct and indirect claims against them held by both local and foreign investors, at least in the short run.

As a general rule, the consequences of fiscal crises are most severe for a government's implicit obligations to residents, such as assets denominated in the local currency, and risky private-to-private, cross-border claims, such as portfolio and direct foreign investment, and less severe for external sovereign obligations, which are explicit in that they are denominated in a currency other than that of the borrower (Lessard 1987, Magee and Brock 1986). The reason for this is that the enforceability of any particular claim depends on the trade-off between the benefits of default and the sanctions that it would trigger. A default on foreign obligations might induce collective action imposing a partial or total cutoff of international trade and finance, while a default on implicit domestic obligations will typically involve fewer immediate sanctions, although it will result in a further stimulus to capital

---

11. See Kraft (1984) for a discussion of the rescue of Mexico's external obligations.

flight, higher domestic real interest rates, a consequent reduction in capital formation, and perhaps a loss of domestic political support.

The result of this greater exposure of implicit domestic claims is that up to a point an increase in country risk is likely to induce capital flight, as cross-border sovereign claims that represent explicit, general obligations of the state are substituted for implicit domestic claims.[12] This substitution is triggered by residents' recognition that these domestic claims are effectively subordinated to the external sovereign obligations.[13] But private local and foreign investment is discouraged by the uncertainty over macroeconomic and regulatory policies precipitated inter alia by concerns over a growing external debt burden. At some point, all claims become extremely risky and voluntary flows cease.

With hindsight, severe debt problems and capital flight in developing countries have often involved a slippery slope. To increase or maintain domestic consumption in the face of external shocks, or to increase the power of the state in allocating resources,[14] the sovereign borrowed abroad, increasing its future fiscal and foreign-exchange requirements. In some cases the borrowing was used to finance productive investment that would generate returns to pay the debt service, but in other cases it was not. In reaction to an internal or external shock, and in some instances in response to external pressure, the state absorbed a significant proportion of the external obligations of the private sector to prevent failures that would have reduced domestic confidence or violated its implicit or explicit guarantees to foreign lenders, thus increasing its fiscal and foreign-exchange burden. Then private claimants, recognizing their subordination to increased foreign claims on the sovereign, often as a result of the violation of some implicit contract by the increasingly

---

12. Implicit domestic claims include assets denominated in the local currency, assets redeemable only in the local jurisdiction regardless of their currency of denomination, and equity and quasi-equity claims on local firms whose value depends on implicit claims on the sovereign. For an excellent discussion of the relative risk of a sovereign's explicit foreign obligations and its implicit domestic obligations, see Protopapadakis (1985).
13. For a rigorous development of this argument, see Ize and Ortiz (1986) and Eaton (1987). Gennotte, Kharas, and Sadeq (1987) demonstrate some of the implications of the resulting conflicts among senior and junior claimants, although their primary focus is on the conflict between first-tier creditors, including the IMF and the World Bank, and second-tier commercial bank creditors, rather than between these two taken together and domestic claimants.
14. Frieden (1981) has argued compellingly that many developing countries used external finance to increase the state's sphere of influence in the domestic economy.

pressed sovereign, seek to transfer assets to other jurisdictions. In the absence of a securities market where such attempted transfers depress asset prices and, hence, face an implicit penalty, these attempted transfers create a run on foreign exchange reserves, forcing either further foreign borrowing (and subordination of private claims) or some form of default on existing claims. Variations on this theme have occurred in most Latin American countries.

The likelihood and severity of such crises are increased by opportunistic behavior on the part of source-country residents, who arrange their financial affairs so as to reduce their exposure to these policy responses as well as to exploit arbitrage opportunities resulting from government interventions that are typical in such crisis periods. This behavior involves shifting funds abroad and simultaneously increasing the proportion of domestic undertakings financed by external credit, which are likely to be "socialized" when the going gets rough. Therefore, capital flight is both a cause and an effect of fiscal instability, creating a vicious circle that is extremely hard to break.

Empirical Findings

Cuddington (ch. 4) estimates the causes of capital flight for four major flight countries—Argentina, Mexico, Uruguay, and Venezuela. His model, like most others of the investment-climate variety, is a portfolio model—where a representative investor allocates his wealth among various assets based on their relative returns and risks. Using nine annual observations, he estimates the extent to which resident capital outflow is statistically explained by several variables: the expected rate of depreciation (the difference between the current real exchange rate and its long-run average) plus the foreign interest rate, the domestic interest rate, expected domestic inflation, and disbursement of public and publicly guaranteed loans.

In the case of Mexico, Cuddington finds a significant correlation between capital flight and overvaluation, disbursements of public debt, and lagged capital flight. He interprets these results as suggesting that the fear of devaluation is a major "driver" of flight in this case and that foreign lending did provide liquidity to support the flight. His estimate of the "propensity to flee" with respect to additional sovereign external borrowing is 0.31. In other words, 31 cents out of a dollar lent by foreign creditors leave the country in the form of capital flight! Foreign interest rates did not enter his final equation, but he argues that this could be due to their relatively high correlation with disbursements.

In the case of Argentina, the only variables remaining in his final fitted model are the lagged real effective exchange rate and the error of the model in prior periods.[15] This he interprets as suggesting that exchange rate expectations are the primary drivers of capital flight in Argentina, and that disbursements and foreign interest rates played no significant role. The results for Uruguay are very similar. In the case of Venezuela, overvaluation and foreign interest rates both enter into the explanation.

Conesa (1986) estimated a similar model with 16 data points.[16] While his findings also vary from country to country, he identifies six major causes of capital flight: lack of economic growth in the source country; an overvalued exchange rate; a high US (nominal) interest rate; local inflation; an excessive fiscal deficit; and (with ambiguous results) the real local interest rate. In theory, the association between (a lack of) growth and capital flight could go in either direction. A lack of growth could signal a lack of attractive investment opportunities, while capital flight, whatever its motivation, can be expected to reduce growth. Conesa argues convincingly that the causation runs from growth to flight. In contrast with Cuddington, Conesa does not attempt to estimate overvaluation relative to some equilibrium exchange rate. Rather, he uses the level of government external borrowings and reserves as proxies for overvaluation, arguing that they permit overvaluation to occur. Further, he claims that the real exchange rate by itself has limited explanatory power.

Studies of the discriminatory-treatment variety emphasize those factors that cause expected asset returns to residents to diverge from the underlying social returns and from expected returns offered nonresidents. Dooley, for example, does not seek to model residents' full portfolio choice. Rather, he focuses on ways that source countries explicitly or implicitly impose

---

15. This model was estimated using annual data. Cuddington notes that in his other work, using quarterly data, the current exchange rate enters as well.

16. A major limitation with the empirical estimates reported here and elsewhere is the very small number of observations available if one relies on balance of payments figures. In an attempt to overcome this limitation, Conesa related capital flight to each of the six factors one by one, and decided which factors were important on the basis of the results of each bivariate regression. Unfortunately this procedure has serious statistical difficulties, which make the results unreliable. Several conference participants suggested that greater attention be given to time series, such as foreign bank deposits in the United States which, although incomplete in scope, are reported with greater frequency. Another suggestion for future work was the use of pooled cross-section, time-series data.

discriminatory "taxes" on domestic asset holders, where the taxes are interpreted broadly to include not only outright taxes, but also takings through inflation, interest ceilings, or multiple exchange rates. He estimates capital flight as a function of three independent variables: inflation—capturing the "inflation tax" on domestic noninterest-bearing monetary assets; financial repression—a measure of the degree to which domestic yields are held below "market-clearing" levels; and a country-risk variable that attempts to measure the riskiness of a country's obligations to the rest of the world relative to that of its claims on the rest of the world. He finds that all three are significantly related to capital flight.

Cuddington's results taken as a whole, supplemented by Conesa's similar results, tell a story of capital flight that is in large part the result of macroeconomic mismanagement—especially exchange rate overvaluation, but also at least by implication high inflation and fiscal deficits. Dooley's more narrowly focused results also point to macroeconomic errors, albeit in the form of inflation, financial repression, and a general measure of country risk.

One notable omission from all the studies are estimates of the impact of exchange controls on capital flight. While Brazil and Colombia, which maintained such controls, experienced proportionately less flight than the other major Latin countries, this could be attributed either to the controls themselves, the macroeconomic policies made possible because of the controls, or factors totally unrelated to the controls. Cuddington's approach of estimating separate equations for each country could not have picked up the effect of controls remaining in force throughout the period studied. Further, he did not include these two countries. Dooley, in contrast, employed a cross-sectional approach, but he did not include capital controls as a factor.

The results described above are not as dissimilar as the contrast between the investment climate and discriminatory treatment hypotheses might have led one to expect. As noted by Khan and Ul Haque (1985), all of these phenomena—overvaluation, inflation, and financial repression—are often symptoms of a country that is fiscally overextended, although Venezuela provides an exception. In reviewing the Argentine case, Dornbusch (1985) states that the

> . . .source of capital flight was a combination of currency overvaluation, the threat of devaluation, and ongoing and increasing financial instability. The domestic instability derives from an inability to bring deficits under control and [to] stop the inflationary process in a decisive way.

Eaton (1987) reinterprets this in terms of a tax on resident claims, stressing that

The [Argentine] government's inability to finance expenditure, including debt service obligations, led to inflationary finance, a form of taxation of domestic capital. As a consequence, capital fled.

Perhaps the greatest difference between the two perspectives lies in their interpretation of the role of loan disbursements. In the investment-climate hypothesis, new loans permit a relaxation in policy that allows residents to satisfy their desire to place funds abroad. In the discriminatory treatment hypothesis, in contrast, a vicious circle can be triggered either by an increased desire of residents to place funds abroad or by an increase in external borrowings, with larger outflows stimulating additional borrowing and extra borrowing increasing the concern of residents about the probability of an impending crisis.

Viewed in that light, one surely has to conclude that both perspectives can help to explain events of recent years. The most rapid resident accumulation of foreign assets occurred while countries were getting themselves into trouble, but still faced an elastic supply of foreign exchange through sovereign borrowing since the risks to external creditors appeared appreciably less than those to domestic residents. But capital outflows persisted after voluntary external lending had ceased, in response to an increase in country-risk levels to the point where even sovereign claims were jeopardized, which can hardly be explained by the discriminatory treatment hypothesis.

4 Consequences

In the case of a country without exchange controls, where capital flight takes place through the official market, its immediate consequence is to reduce the level of foreign-exchange reserves or to require increased foreign borrowing. When any excess reserves and unused borrowing capacity have been used up so that the foreign-exchange constraint starts to bite, the country will be obliged to initiate balance of payments adjustment. At best, this will involve devaluation (or equivalent measures) to switch purchases of tradables from foreign to domestic sources, thus absorbing resources that would otherwise have been available for domestic investment into the generation of a current account surplus to pay for the capital flight. At worst, adjustment will take place not by expenditure switching but by expenditure reduction—by reducing demand, and with it output, to whatever point is needed to cut the demand for imports enough to transform capital outflow into current account surplus.

Thus, the best case involves a reduction in the savings to finance domestic investment, of a magnitude essentially[17] equal to the size of the capital flight. Future growth will in consequence be lower. The worst case involves a reduction not just in future growth possibilities but also in the current level of output, by some *multiple*[18] of the size of capital flight. This decline in output will typically have a high component of investment, either because the government finds cuts in public investment the easiest to make, or because it deliberately seeks to squeeze import-intensive activities, or because of the adverse effects of recession on business confidence. Thus, future growth potential is likely to decline, as well as current output, by even more than in the "best case." In the best case, the savings constraint is tightened and reduces future growth possibilities; in the worst case, the foreign exchange constraint imposes both a larger cutback in future growth and a loss in current output.[19] The typical case is presumably intermediate, with some expenditure switching (hopefully in increasing proportion) limiting the necessary short-run decline in output, but a cut in investment at least as large as the magnitude of capital outflow.

To set against those losses, one must weigh the foreign interest income earned by those who placed capital abroad. In the best case, where the loss of future domestic income is equal to the marginal product of capital (times the capital outflow), society as a whole will gain if the rate of return on foreign assets exceeds the marginal product of domestic investment, and lose in the converse case. A simple-minded neoclassical view would be that this

---

17. If devaluation has an adverse impact on the terms of trade, the decline in resource availability and therefore in the potential level of investment will be somewhat larger. But the difference is likely to be extremely modest in developing countries, which rarely have much monopoly (let alone monopsony) power in international trade in the medium term.
18. The foreign-trade multiplier analysis shows that the necessary decline in income is $(1/m)$ times the needed improvement in the trade balance, where m is the marginal propensity to import, a fraction. See Williamson (1983, section 8.2).
19. The analysis is that of the two-gap model. See Williamson (1983, section 12.3).

implies that foreign investment will occur if and only if it is socially advantageous, for why would investors place their funds abroad if they did not anticipate a higher rate of return?

In fact, however, there are strong reasons for expecting the economic return on domestic investment to exceed the economic rate of return to the source country on foreign assets, especially in the context of capital flight. In the first place, capital is relatively scarce in developing countries, and hence there is a presumption that, unless policies cause extreme distortions, its marginal product will be higher there. Second, the rate of return on real capital typically exceeds that on financial assets, since it includes returns to managers and entrepreneurs to compensate for the trouble and risk of undertaking real investment. Third, some part of the return to domestic capital formation accrues to workers (in the form of higher wages) and consumers (in the form of better and cheaper products) rather than to the investors. Fourth, investors normally pay taxes on interest and profits generated at home, whereas that earned abroad is usually de facto tax-free (of foreign as well as domestic taxes). Finally, when output is constrained by the shortage of foreign exchange, the economic cost of the loss of a dollar of foreign exchange is much greater than the cost of one less dollar of investment, as explained above by the two-gap analysis.[20]

Thus, there are strong reasons for expecting the economic return on the displaced domestic investment to exceed the return earned on the foreign investments bought by the funds that flee. This does not contradict the expectation that private investors will shift funds abroad only if they perceive the risk-adjusted return to be higher there, because all of the above factors except the first involve a wedge between the economic return on investment and the financial return to the investor, and it is, of course, the latter that drives private investment decisions. Indeed, there is yet another reason why foreign investment may appear more attractive to individual wealth-owners

---

20. We are, however, somewhat dubious of the argument that the returns on foreign investments can be dismissed because the funds "never come back." If those investments proved extremely lucrative and their owners spent all the profits abroad, it is not obvious that this is worse from a national perspective than to have the wealth-owners make equally profitable investments with zero spillover benefits at home and then take the proceeds abroad to spend. An egalitarian may not regard the outcome as contributing much to national welfare, but this is because the income accrues to the rich (we would feel differently if the proceeds were used to give educational foreign trips to orphans) rather than because it is "lost to the country."

than it does to their society, namely that many of the risks they are seeking to escape—such as expropriation or devaluation—involve a redistribution of income at the expense of the wealth-owners rather than a net loss to the society.

The conclusion that developing countries are harmed by capital flight does not imply that developed countries could expect to benefit by restricting capital outflows. For example, capital is typically not a scarce factor in developed countries. Neither do developed countries typically suffer from a foreign-exchange constraint, any more than they do from acute fears of expropriation or massive devaluation. Furthermore, the existence of double taxation treaties, with their provisions for information exchange, makes it somewhat less likely that taxes can be avoided by holding funds abroad. It is still true that real domestic investment is to be preferred to foreign financial investment inasmuch as real investment produces returns that accrue to other agents besides the owners of capital, but most developed countries probably gain practically as much from those benefits yielded by inward direct investment as they lose from the outward investment they permit. In sum, capital mobility seems a sensible enough policy for the typical developed country, but this does not imply that the same is true for a natural capital importer.

The preceding analysis is based on the "two-gap model," the classic tool for analyzing the impact of a change in foreign-exchange availability on a developing country.[21] It has been argued that the standard conclusions of that model—namely, that a loss of foreign exchange is disadvantageous, and that this is particularly true when it creates a foreign-exchange constraint independent of the savings constraint—apply as much to losses caused by

---

21. The analysis assumed that capital outflows were legal and therefore took place through the official foreign exchange market. It is interesting to ask what difference it makes when exchange controls prohibit the placement of funds abroad and therefore capital flight has to take place through a parallel or black market. The proximate effect will be to increase the premium on the dollar in the black market. This will divert some sales of foreign exchange from the official to the black market, for example, by promoting misinvoicing (Gulati, ch. 3), or by encouraging smuggling; to that extent, the effects will be the same as if there were no black market. It is also likely to stimulate some export sales that would not otherwise have taken place and whose proceeds can be realized in the black market. This will preempt resources as in the analysis of the savings-constrained case when the economy is fully employed, but when there is unemployment it will promote additional output. The distributional and other effects discussed below will be absent or much attenuated.

capital flight as to any others. But, in a provocative paper, Rodriguez (ch. 6) argues that the effects of capital flight are far more corrosive than this.

He points out that it is the wealthy who had, and exploited, the opportunity to place funds abroad during the years when capital flight was motivated by discriminatory treatment. Those dollars were bought at subsidized rates (in the days of overvalued exchange rates). In some cases the state was simultaneously subsidizing domestic investments undertaken by those same individuals, while state enterprises were then pushed into foreign borrowing in order to satisfy the public-sector budget constraint. In other cases the private sector borrowed abroad on behalf of its productive enterprises at the same time that it was building up dollar bank deposits in its private capacity. In both cases, even before any of the problems discussed above that result from a shortage of savings or foreign exchange had materialized, the local economy had begun to suffer from a shift of financial intermediation offshore and consequent stultification of the development of the local capital market.

However, matters worsened dramatically when the debt crisis cut off access to new foreign borrowing. Since the foreign assets held by the private sector did not generate any dollar income for the source country but the foreign debts had to be serviced in dollars, balance of payments adjustment became necessary. This involved large real devaluations, which enriched holders of dollar assets and impoverished those with dollar liabilities. Even where those liabilities had originally been incurred by the private sector, they were soon de facto nationalized, either directly or indirectly (via the provision of foreign exchange to make interest payments at privileged rates), in some cases under foreign pressure but in many cases apparently without any serious consideration of the alternative of allowing the indebted enterprises to go bankrupt. This might well have induced the return of some of the flight capital (to keep the enterprises solvent), while in other cases it would have reduced the foreign debt and permitted reorganization under new management, public or private, domestic or foreign. In fact, government help in servicing foreign debt, by the provision of foreign exchange at a special exchange rate, on occasion tended to deter repatriation, inasmuch as the owners might have feared that repatriation would provoke offsetting claims. The one country to flirt with the straightforward capitalist solution of allowing bankruptcy was Chile, which was quickly forced to nationalize its foreign debts by its commercial bank creditors, on pain of withdrawal of trade credit. Rumor has it that oil tankers bound for Chile turned around, and the government capitulated within 24 hours (Arellano and Ramos, ch. 7, n. 4).

The process everywhere ended up with the public sector owing the dollar debts and the wealthy owning private dollar assets. The public sector's enlarged obligations pushed it into structural deficit, from which all the efforts toward fiscal austerity have not yet rescued it. The burden of fiscal austerity is borne by the less wealthy segments of society, who did not have the resources to place their funds abroad beyond the reach of taxation. The fiscal gap is filled by the inflation tax. The net impact is a regressive redistribution of income and wealth on a massive scale.

Hence the consequences of capital flight include not just the macroeconomic costs of lost output and curtailed future growth opportunities, but also the exportation of financial intermediation, perverse redistribution of income, structural budget deficits, and inflation. But Rodriguez argues that even this is not the end of the story. Domestic capitalists who find themselves with a large part of their wealth abroad for a lengthy period are tempted to start looking for more challenging investment opportunities than passive ownership of financial assets and real estate. They start taking over corporations in the developed countries, and before long not just their wealth but their entrepreneurial energies and their economic stake in national policies are lost to their native societies. In this vision the whole future of the development process is jeopardized by capital flight.

5 Source-Country Policies

The principal responsibility for stemming resident capital outflows inevitably falls on the source countries, since there is no question but that their own inadequate policies were the primary source of the problem. To defend their interests, the wealthy reacted to those policy failings, but this merely emphasizes that policy should always be designed on the assumption that that is how those with the ability to do so will behave. The present section examines what countries need to do to "set their house in order" so as to ensure that capital flight does not recur.

Macroeconomic Fundamentals

In the final paragraph of his historical survey of capital flight, Charles Kindleberger (ch. 2) recalled a 1937 memo of his which:

. . . laid heavy emphasis on the restoration of confidence. Such restoration, it was thought, might precede or follow renewed domestic investment and economic recovery . . . but excluded further depreciation. . . . This essentially means that short-run measures in the foreign exchange market, such as a stabilization or a squeeze, must be buttressed by long-run macroeconomic stabilization that is seen to be politically supportable. It is quite an order.

The conclusion that, however difficult the task, macroeconomic policy needs to be firmly set on a sustainable course, if there is to be any chance of containing capital outflows, was one of the few propositions to win general consent during the Institute's conference. Confidence in the sustainability of macroeconomic policy is unlikely in the absence of a realistic exchange rate, a positive but moderate real interest rate, robust economic growth, and a medium-run resolution of the debt problem.

Cuddington (ch. 4) provides strong evidence that an overvalued exchange rate is a prime cause of capital flight, a result that confirms intuition and much anecdotal evidence.[22] If a government wishes to control capital flight, it must break with the bad habit of allowing its currency to become overvalued. This may be accomplished either by allowing the currency to float or by setting it at a realistic level and then making sure that the real exchange rate is not appreciated by high domestic inflation. It is vital to gain public confidence that this policy will be maintained, even in the event of political change. Without this certainty, exporters will lack the incentive to invest, and hence the trade adjustments needed to sustain the policy are unlikely to materialize.

A sensible interest-rate policy is also of key importance, although for technical reasons (namely, the problem of reverse causation) Cuddington was unable to provide econometric evidence to buttress this claim. The aim should be a dependably positive real interest rate that is somewhat above the

---

22. This is not to say that an overvalued exchange rate is always associated with capital flight. On the contrary, misplaced confidence may well cause or sustain overvaluation for a time—as happened in Britain in 1980–81, in the United States in 1982–85, and in Chile in 1981 (an episode explored by Arellano and Ramos, ch. 7).

international rate even after allowing for any depreciation of the domestic currency needed to preserve competitiveness. But it is important that the interest rate not be too high as well as that it not be too low. An excessively high interest rate discourages productive investment and can even jeopardize the financial viability of existing productive enterprises. It also raises the problem of adverse selection: that is, only entrepreneurs with speculative projects in mind are prepared to borrow, comforted by the thought that the lender will bear a part of the cost if the project fails. An economy where the financial markets have been reduced to gambling casinos is all too prone to generate capital flight, as shown by Argentine experience in the early 1980s.

It is also plausible that economic growth will help to reduce capital flight, by generating confidence in the domestic economy, opening up attractive investment opportunities, and allowing the economy to pay remunerative interest and profit returns without cutting real wages to a point that would generate social unrest. Indeed, Conesa (1986) reports evidence of such an effect: according to his analysis, growth is actually the most important single deterrent to capital flight. Of course, growth is not a policy variable in the direct way that exchange and interest rates are, but the conclusion that growth helps deter capital flight nevertheless provides another reason for welcoming the pro-growth bias of official policy since the conception of the Baker Plan, and for avoiding excessive austerity in IMF programs. Likewise, this conclusion provides another reason for supporting supply-oriented adjustment measures—including market liberalization, fiscal reform, debureaucratization, and outward orientation, as Balassa et al. (1986) urge—as well as the longer term approach to debt rescheduling that at last seems on the road to implementation.

The proposition that realistic exchange rates, positive but reasonable real interest rates, and a resumption of growth are necessary to master capital flight seems to be rather uncontroversial. Where controversy still rages is on whether "getting the fundamentals right" is just a necessary or is also a sufficient condition for dealing with capital flight.

This question deserves a qualified answer. It may well be that a full restoration of confidence, including confidence in the permanence of the new policy stance in the face of possible political change as well as establishment of realistic exchange and interest rates and a resumption of growth, would suffice to induce a return of flight capital.

The problem with this conclusion is that it does not explain how to break out of the vicious circle of low growth, capital flight, foreign-exchange constraint, and thus continued low growth. Mere changes in macroeconomic policy may not permit the restoration of growth until the foreign-exchange constraint is broken, while capital flight will not go into reverse and help break the foreign-exchange constraint until growth resumes. Very tight credit policies may help bring capital back, as in Mexico recently, but they are hardly calculated to restore growth. Moreover, confidence in the future may be very hard for a government to engineer, no matter how well-intentioned it may be, if only because that confidence depends also on perceptions of the likely actions of its political opponents. In an intermediate situation where current policies merit confidence but the long-term outlook remains problematic, the array of other policies discussed below can be of especial importance.

Corruption

In many countries it may not be just a change in macroeconomic policy that is needed to master capital flight but also a change in the ethics of those involved in public life. No matter how attractive domestic economic prospects, anyone who derives illicit income from bribes on public-sector contracts or from the award of import licenses is likely to wish to place at least some of the resulting assets abroad (see Walter, ch. 5). And a correction of the tax distortions that currently provide an incentive to place funds abroad (see below) is hardly likely if the officials who would have to negotiate a tax treaty attach greater importance to their private interest in retaining tax-exempt, foreign nest-eggs than to the social interest in achieving tax neutrality. A society that lacks the social cohesion to ensure that its leaders place public duties ahead of personal gain may well be condemned to repeated bouts of capital flight.

Of course, policy changes can significantly reduce the incentives for corruption. Ending the rationing of underpriced foreign exchange or credit would remove some of the major sources of gain from such behavior. However, such policies are not always mere miscalculations. They are major sources of state power, and they are unlikely to be definitively changed until there is both a public awareness of their distorting, demoralizing effects and a political commitment to honest government.

This is a delicate subject, on which foreign preaching is unlikely to achieve much. Indeed, if preaching is not to be counterproductive, it is important that the preachers not pose as more self-righteous than their own actions justify. At the same time, neither the delicacy of the subject nor the lack of reliable estimates of the social cost of corruption should deter one from recognizing the pervasiveness of the problem and the urgency of those societies' coming to terms with it. Perhaps the most useful thing that outsiders can do is to support the efforts of countries (like the Philippines) that show signs of trying to escape from the debilitating grip of pervasive corruption.

Domestic Financial Markets

As well as establishing credible, consistent macroeconomic policies, source countries need to undertake major changes in their treatment of domestic financial intermediation in order to avoid an excessive gap between the economic returns provided by the underlying economic prospects and the returns that private investors can reasonably expect to earn. At the same time, they must limit their fiscal exposure to private losses in order to increase their ability to maintain consistent policies.

Source-country governments have to recognize that they are engaged in international competition for capital. Hence, they must avoid viewing domestic savings as captive resources that can be taxed and allocated at will. As noted in our discussion of the causes of capital flight, source-country residents face numerous explicit and implicit taxes and fiscal risks when investing in domestic securities and business activities. Passive income from wealth is often (though by no means always) taxed at high rates relative to world average levels, both because of high statutory rates and the increase in effective rates that results from inflation. Further, the rate payable on formal savings instruments, especially bank deposits, is often limited by law to nominal levels that result in low or negative real returns. This financial repression is an implicit tax on savings that is typically passed on to the government or to government-favored sectors through reserve requirements and direct lending at controlled rates. Even where interest rates are not controlled, noninterest-bearing reserve requirements coupled with inflation act as a tax on domestic financial intermediation. In order not to erode the "tax base," these taxes have to be coupled with limits on currency convertibility (which can be avoided only through illegal capital flight).

Potential changes in explicit and implicit taxes on financial intermediation are also a major source of financial risk. In periods of overall financial crisis, these are often the only mechanisms through which governments can increase revenues in the short run, either by tightening restrictions or simply by printing money and imposing an inflation tax that falls primarily on financial intermediation. Thus, even though a government may have a policy goal of providing residents with internationally competitive returns on savings, this policy will not be credible if there is a significant chance of an overall fiscal crisis.

While fiscal crises threaten domestic financial intermediation, the structure of that intermediation often contributes to the potential for such crises, creating a vicious circle. Governments are often compelled to intervene to maintain the viability of both public and private enterprises and, particularly, financial institutions that incur significant losses.[23] This problem is exacerbated in many developing countries, including most of the major sources of capital flight, by their heavy reliance on bank or nonbank intermediaries that issue primarily liquid, supposedly default-free, securities. *A la par y a la vista,* at par on sight, are the terms not only for bank deposits but also for the liabilities of nonbank intermediaries such as *financieras,* which represent the bulk of financial assets held by households in many Latin American countries. Government intervention to maintain these terms has played key roles in recent internal financial crises in Argentina, Chile, Mexico, and Venezuela, among others.

With such "house of cards" structures, any significant asset loss can trigger a collapse of the financial sector with the attendant social costs. The fact that the government is committed to intervene in the case of major losses encourages opportunistic behavior in the financial sector, since the value of the implicit call on government resources is an increasing function of the potential variability of the assets it holds.[24] This tendency is typically exacerbated by lax controls over self-dealing by private financial institutions, allowing scoundrels to borrow from banks they control directly or indirectly at (excessively low) rates that reflect depositors' faith that the government will make good on the claims in the case of private failure.

Any event that increases the perceived risk of a financial crisis is likely to trigger a run on the domestic financial system since the value of deposits

---

23. See Gillis, Lessard, and Jenkins (1982) for further development of this point in the case of state-owned enterprises, whose growth was promoted by foreign borrowing in many developing countries.

24. Merton (1977) provides the pioneering analysis of this phenomenon.

remains fixed in the short run. This, in turn, will reduce tax revenues, further weakening the fiscal situation. If exchange rates are also stabilized in the short run, this run on the system takes the form of capital flight.

The negative consequences of these financial dynamics are readily apparent. Because of the distortions introduced by present and possible future interventions, the system fails to allocate resources properly. It is crisis prone, and crises, and even expectations of crises, are likely to trigger capital flight.

In the light of these complex interactions, removing financial repression is a necessary but not a sufficient condition for restoring stable, viable patterns of domestic intermediation in developing countries. Financial markets need to be broadened and deepened so that a much larger proportion of the risks implicit in real investments are passed through to investors in the form of securities whose price can vary in line with the perceived value of the underlying assets. This requires strengthening the capital base of the financial sector to allow it to absorb greater fluctuations in asset values; improving bank regulation to ensure that bank shareholders rather than society bear these residual risks; and increasing the role of bond and equity financing.

Such reforms are difficult to accomplish, although a number of countries are now looking at the question very seriously. Improving bank regulation involves a difficult balancing act. On the one hand, the government must signal its commitment to maintaining the value of deposits and the solvency of the system. On the other hand, it must do so in a way that does not encourage opportunistic behavior that increases the state's risk exposure.

Deepening financial markets requires a coherent and appropriate body of corporate and securities law. In many cases, it also requires reforms in tax statutes and improvement in tax enforcement, since, in practice, most developing-country tax systems discriminate against formal financial intermediation, whether through banks or through equity markets. Effective reforms will typically include a reduction of taxes on capital gains or, at a minimum, price-level indexing to determine gains, and the elimination of special wealth taxes on securities.

Exchange Control

Among the Latin American countries, at least, there is an exact correspondence between the countries that had no exchange control at the turn of the decade and those that suffered capital flight on a massive scale. Argentina, Mexico,

Uruguay, and Venezuela all experienced massive outflows; in all of them the outflows were perfectly legal. In contrast, outflows were relatively modest from Brazil, Chile, Colombia, and Peru, all of which maintained restrictions on capital outflows that made the accumulation of foreign assets illegal. (One cannot, however, be sure that the outflows were quite as modest as the figures suggest, since the very fact that capital transfers are illegal tends to ensure that capital flight takes forms that are harder to trace.) Korea and the Philippines, which both maintained exchange controls and experienced minimal and modest outflows, respectively, also fit the pattern.

This contrast makes it difficult to justify policy advice to debtor countries to dismantle an existing system of exchange controls. Moreover, the welfare gain from allowing private citizens unimpeded access to world capital markets comes primarily from the opportunity this gives *creditors* to choose a portfolio that suits their preferences in terms of rewards and risks. But for a *debtor* country, allowing citizens to invest abroad means either increasing its financial exposure by borrowing more or curtailing its absorption of real resources. In either event, the social loss has to be weighed against the private gain of the investor. Admittedly, some libertarians argue that the freedom to invest is a right that should not be circumscribed by "nationalistic" conceptions of the impact on social welfare, but an egalitarian can retort that the gainers from free capital movements are virtually certain to be richer than the losers.

In addition, a more concrete objection exists to a policy of preventing capital outflows, assuming this to be feasible. Especially in countries with exposure to a few commodities or industries, constraining residents to hold only domestic assets will impose on them large but potentially diversifiable risks. If the opening of markets to capital flows would result in inflows to offset the outflows, the country would gain relative to being closed. However, there is little evidence that the cross flows for diversification actually take place, except in the past in the form of bank debt which placed excessive risk on the debtor. The interest now being shown in "emerging market" equities by investors in developed countries is, however, a hopeful sign that things may be changing.

In view of these conflicting considerations, the decision as to whether to maintain exchange controls surely falls within the area of legitimate national discretion, provided that a country that decides to maintain controls also makes a credible commitment to resist the potential for increased opportunism on the part of the government. It would certainly be an error to imagine that exchange controls offer some sort of panacea. Many countries have imposed exchange controls but have failed to make them work, including Mexico (not to mention France) in 1982. And the reason that some countries managed to avoid massive capital flight is not merely because they made it illegal. Brazil offered attractive indexed domestic assets and kept the exchange rate competitive; Chile liberalized its trade account to a point where it was easier to shift into durable goods than into foreign financial assets; Colombia had a stream of illegal foreign earnings that permitted accumulation of foreign financial assets without anything that showed up as capital flight in the statistics; and Peru provided domestic dollar-denominated assets. Absent those factors, it is entirely possible that these countries would have experienced major capital flight even with exchange control. Indeed, Brazil appears to have developed a nonnegligible volume of capital flight after 1982.

Moreover, exchange controls cannot be used to induce a return of flight capital. On the contrary, experience shows that imposition of exchange controls deters a reflux of capital and that their removal encourages such a return. This is not surprising, since an important motive for shifting funds abroad is to ensure their ready availability in terms of foreign exchange.

Perhaps the most sensible attitude is that of Miguel Urrutia (ch. 8) in his defense of Colombian practice. He pointed out that Colombia has maintained capital controls over the years while being careful to ensure that they were not used as a *substitute* for sound policies. Thus, the dollar has sometimes been at a premium and sometimes at a discount on the black market: capital controls have helped to minimize fluctuations in the real exchange rate facing exporters as well as to reduce flows of hot money that might otherwise have destabilized the economy. On average these controls may also have helped to maintain somewhat lower interest rates than would otherwise have been necessary, but they have not been asked to override any major incentive to shift funds abroad.

Provided that not too much is asked of exchange controls, they may be a useful element in the policy arsenal. Capital-importing countries that have a functioning exchange-control system should certainly not be pressed to abolish it. Even countries that have already lost much resident capital may need to ponder the trade-off between reduced chances of attracting it back if exchange controls are imposed versus increased dangers of losing new savings if they are not. Nevertheless, exchange controls will do more harm than good if they are treated as a panacea that can substitute for adequate policies.

Taxation

Capital outflows can be encouraged or discouraged by taxation arrangements in both source and haven countries. We defer until the next section a consideration of the responsibilities of haven countries, and concentrate here on the actions that the source countries need to take in order to remove the tax incentive to place funds abroad.

A distortion encouraging capital outflow arises when the effective rate of taxation on either investment income or wealth is lower on assets held abroad than on those held domestically. This can arise either because the statutory tax liabilities are lower on investment income generated (or wealth held) abroad, or because enforcement of legal obligations is less effective.

As described below, in practice many tax-exempt assets are available to nonresidents in the haven countries. Thus the legal tax obligation faced by a developing-country investor depends primarily on the laws of his home country. These vary enormously, depending on the country's attitude toward the "origin principle" versus the "residence principle" of taxation.[25] Argentina is the extreme case of a country that follows the origin principle. This means that it does not attempt to tax Argentine residents' investment income generated, nor wealth held, outside Argentina. But since it does tax the increase in wealth held in Argentina as well as investment income earned in Argentina, Argentine residents face a strong tax incentive to place funds abroad (especially when this enables them to avoid showing an increase in wealth held in Argentina on their tax returns). These incentives are actually stronger the more scrupulous a taxpayer is in fulfilling his legal obligation to declare the increase in his Argentine-held wealth.

Venezuela provides a good example of a country that has recently embraced the residence principle of taxation. While it still permits the ownership of foreign assets, it has passed a law requiring the registration of foreign investments and the declaration of income on them for tax purposes (taxable at the rather modest rate of 14 percent). If all taxpayers were completely

---

25. The "origin principle" (or "source basis") of taxation, referred to by tax lawyers as an exclusively territorial concept of taxation, involves an attempt to tax exclusively the income generated within a certain country (the components of GDP). The "residence principle" involves an attempt to tax the income generated anywhere in the world that accrues to the residents of a particular country (i.e., the components of GNP), referred to by tax lawyers as an extraterritorial or global concept of taxation.

honest and the tax rate were the same on domestic and foreign income, the tax incentive to hold assets abroad rather than at home would be eliminated.

Since, however, many taxpayers declare income only when they believe the tax authority can police their compliance, the tax incentive would in fact be eliminated only if enforcement were equally effective with respect to interest income earned abroad rather than at home. This is by no means the case. Among the developing countries of the Western Hemisphere, only a few small Caribbean countries[26] have tax treaties with the United States that entitle them to information-sharing with the US tax authorities. Without an information-sharing agreement with the major haven countries, foremost the United States, the possibility of effective enforcement of taxes on investment income earned abroad is virtually nonexistent.

Two distinct policy initiatives are therefore called for if the developing countries are to eliminate the tax incentive to place funds abroad.

First, for the reasons analyzed above, many developing countries need to reform their own tax laws so as to replace the origin principle (which used to be in their national self-interest, for reasons noted below) by the residence principle. This may not accomplish much alone, but without this step all else is futile.

Second, they need to establish information-sharing agreements with the principal haven countries. This has traditionally been done as a part of tax treaties. Latin countries have, however, held back from signing tax treaties with the United States. Honduras signed a treaty in 1956, but it was abrogated long ago. Brazil commenced negotiations in 1967 that dragged on until 1981, in which year the US Senate ratified the resulting treaty (and a similar treaty with Argentina). Both Argentina and Brazil refused to reciprocate the ratification, however, in view of changes made by the Senate.

At least two factors underlie this failure. The immediate cause of the refusal of Argentina and Brazil to ratify the tax treaties so laboriously negotiated was the Senate's deletion of "tax-sparing" provisions. Tax sparing

---

26. The United States has encouraged countries to conclude tax treaties within the context of the Caribbean Basin Initiative, prior to which it had a treaty only with the Netherlands Antilles. (In July 1987 the United States announced its intention of terminating this treaty because of an inability to agree on the restrictions that should apply to residents of third countries, but subsequently found that this raised more complex problems than it realized.) Tax treaties with Barbados, Jamaica, and Trinidad and Tobago are now operational, while one with Costa Rica is under negotiation.

involves an agreement by one party that a tax concession made by the other (normally to attract investment) will be treated as a tax credit rather than an increase in taxable income. France, Germany, Japan, and Sweden have all concluded tax treaties with Argentina and Brazil that allow tax sparing for the incentives provided to attract direct investment. Without a similar feature in the tax treaty with the United States, both countries felt that the arrangement they were being offered was unacceptably one-sided.[27]

A more general factor that has militated against the conclusion of tax treaties is the Latin attachment to the origin principle. This principle used to be very clearly in the self-interest of the Latins: as large net foreign debtors on private account (with GDP exceeding GNP), they could gain revenue by taxing the profits earned by multinationals. Indeed, they used the principle to justify (or rationalize, some might claim) a practice of combining corporate and withholding taxes at rates that ensured that virtually all the tax revenues extracted from multinationals operating in Latin America accrued to the local tax authority rather than to the Treasury of the multinationals' home country. The US attempt, as a part of each tax treaty, to regain some of the tax revenue was one stumbling block to the negotiation of treaties. Naturally, a country committed to the origin principle of taxation sees little advantage in a tax treaty that would help it do what it does not desire to do, namely tax the foreign income of its residents.

Whatever may have been the rights and wrongs of these matters in the past, it seems clear that the Latins are now paying a high price for their refusal to negotiate tax treaties. The avoidance of double taxation that a tax treaty ensures could be expected to help revive direct investment. And, following the big cuts in US tax rates, the benefit of being able to tax foreign corporations has been severely eroded. This means that the incidence of the high tax rates still in force in many Latin countries will fall on the multinational rather than on the US Treasury, limiting the much needed expansion of direct foreign investment despite the otherwise improved investment climate of many countries in the region and their more competitive exchange rates. In contrast, the vast sums now held by Latins in US bank deposits and other instruments have much increased the Latin interest in information sharing.

---

27. The issue of tax sparing has become less important as a result of reductions in marginal tax rates in the United States in recent years. Most firms with foreign operations will now have excess foreign tax credits, and hence will benefit from lower local tax rates.

Latin self-interest therefore demands a reappraisal of their traditional hostility to signing tax treaties.

Some participants at the Institute's conference argued that developing countries should concede their inability to tax investment income (just as, in one view, they should refrain from attempting to hold the post-tax real income of the technocracy below international levels, for fear of provoking a brain drain). But this contention was strongly disputed by participants alarmed at the highly concentrated distribution of income and wealth in many debtor countries, which could only be worsened by abandoning the effort to tax investment income. This would imply even greater pressure on immobile factors of production, especially unskilled labor. Moveover, while such a step would eliminate one motive for capital outflows, it would also reduce the source countries' fiscal strength and thus could actually increase the prospects for crisis-related episodes of capital flight.

In our view, source countries need to be realistic in recognizing that high tax rates on wealth (including inheritance taxes) or investment income will tend to motivate citizens to place funds abroad and seek out tax-exempt assets, but they also need to avoid the defeatism of ceasing even to try to tax income from wealth. Opportunities for emigration and tax evasion are sufficiently important to justify the avoidance of tax rates much above the international norm, but not so ubiquitous as to dictate abandoning the attempt to collect revenues comparable to those levied in the major industrial countries. Countries like Argentina need thoroughgoing tax reform designed to reduce the present very high marginal tax rates and compensate for the effect of this on revenue by widening the tax base.

6 Haven-Country Policies

While the primary responsibility for curbing capital flight falls on the source countries, increasing interdependence implies that the attractiveness of placing funds abroad is also importantly influenced by policies pursued in the countries to which money can flee. We designate these the "haven countries," though without implying that they have deliberately sought to attract funds (in the way that the term "tax haven" implies a conscious attempt to attract clients).

Wealthy individuals throughout the world face a broad array of offshore investment alternatives. As recounted by Walter (ch. 5), such individuals, whether located in Latin America, Europe, or the Middle East, are called on at home by private bankers from the world's premiere institutions and are welcomed in major world financial centers. Some of these are offshore financial centers, such as Geneva, Luxembourg, or Panama, which effectively rent their local jurisdiction as a place through which to invest directly or indirectly in other countries. Others, including New York, London, and now Tokyo, are centers for investment as well as intermediation that compete with the offshore centers at least in terms of taxation, though typically not secrecy.

Each magnet location offers a slightly different mix of advantages, and therefore attracts flight capital of a particular type. The United States, for example, offers substantial tax exemption and, while it does not offer secrecy, it does offer deposit insurance and deep capital markets. Hence a middle-class Mexican or Venezuelan, for example, who holds foreign assets as a hedge against domestic crises but has little or no reason to fear being prosecuted, is likely to find a US bank account as attractive as a Swiss one. An investor more interested in hiding overseas holdings, perhaps because capital transfers are restricted by law or because the wealth was gained illicitly, will find Switzerland or Panama more attractive. A Panama does not offer the same government backing of deposits or depth of capital markets as the United States, but this competitive disadvantage may not hold for branches of European banks that can compete on their own financial strength.

While this shifting of funds conjures up images of drug smugglers moving suitcases of cash, most capital flight seems to take place through normal channels. Latin Americans, in particular, are often in effect dual citizens because of their heritage and extensive international travel for business and pleasure. Maintaining a bank account in Miami or San Diego is commonplace, and often completely legal. Even when exchange controls exist, under normal circumstances foreign bank deposits are readily available through relatives or acquaintances.

Policies in the haven countries influence the incentive for residents of developing countries to place their funds abroad through at least three important channels: through the system of taxation, through deposit-seeking activities by the banks, and through the level of world interest rates. These are discussed in turn, starting with taxation, to continue the analysis initiated above with respect to the policies of the source countries.

Taxation

The taxation of investment income is perhaps the most important way policies of the haven countries may help to suck capital out of developing countries. These policies involve both the taxes the haven countries impose on the investment income of nonresidents and the help they provide developing countries to collect taxes the latter impose on the investment income earned by their residents in the haven countries.

Most developed countries, including the United States, have now abandoned taxation of most nonresident investment income. For example, the United States has long exempted from taxation interest on bank deposits owned by nonresidents: it does not even impose a refundable withholding tax. In 1984, it exempted interest on Treasury securities held by nonresidents from withholding as well—a move swiftly followed by France, Germany, and Japan. Thus, withholding tax is now levied only on nonresident income from sources such as dividends, interest on corporate securities, real estate, and royalties.[28]

The waning of the effort to tax nonresident income seems to have arisen as a joint result of two factors. One is sympathy in most developed countries for the residence principle of taxation, which implies that it is proper to exempt nonresident income. The other is international competition for funds: it is argued that internationally mobile investment funds have so many tax-exempt alternatives that any attempt to impose taxes either raises the return the borrower must pay or squeezes the borrower out of the market.

Many participants in the Institute's conference were extremely critical of the implicit policy of most industrial countries—to allow or even solicit offshore funds for tax-free investment with no questions asked. This erosion of the "global fiscal commons," through beggar-my-neighbor competition among industrial countries, is intensified by the competition from tax havens. The time has surely come to try to reverse this trend. It is doubtful if this can be done piecemeal, given the incentive that each country has to ensure that its tax treatment of nonresident income is at least as favorable as the

---

28. In addition, nonresidents are subject to income tax on income effectively connected with a US trade or business and to capital gains tax on real estate.

international norm. Rather, one needs to think in terms of a treaty within the Organization for Economic Cooperation and Development (OECD) that would commit all the industrial countries to imposing a substantial withholding tax, which would be refundable on presentation of evidence that the recipient had reported any investment income to his national tax authority.

Such a proposal naturally raises a number of questions. Perhaps the most obvious is whether such an agreement would not inevitably be undermined by the existence of tax havens. Provided that all the industrial countries subscribe to the OECD treaty, this fear is exaggerated. The reason is that the tax havens act as intermediaries and need to place abroad virtually all the funds deposited with them. Interest earned on sums lent to the industrial countries could itself be made subject to withholding (since a tax haven cannot sign a tax treaty without ceasing to be a tax haven). In this event a tax haven could afford to pay only a rate of interest equal to the post-withholding-tax rate of return in the industrial countries.

Another question is whether withholding tax should be refundable to residents of countries that had not signed a tax treaty with the country where the interest was earned. Presumably this would not be possible since, in the absence of a tax treaty, there would be no mechanism for ensuring the authenticity of tax returns.

However, a related proposal deserves consideration. Diaz-Alejandro (1984) proposed that the United States should turn over the tax revenue from a withholding tax on the interest paid on the deposits of Latin Americans to the Inter-American Development Bank. While such revenue-sharing may sound visionary, the United States has already accepted the principle in one particular context: the proceeds of assets seized in the course of narcotics control from nationals of countries with which the United States has concluded Mutual Legal Assistance Treaties are shared between the United States and the country whose subjects are involved. This precedent deserves to be built on.

The United States has traditionally favored the conclusion of tax treaties. It and the other haven countries should maintain this positive attitude, inter alia, to permit an exchange of information with the source countries to help them enforce their tax laws. In the past, the main obstacle to the negotiation of such treaties has come from the Latin side, as noted in the previous section. But, now that tax reform has reduced the size of the sums at stake, it might be opportune to reconsider the traditional US hostility to the principle of tax sparing, which would encourage Latin willingness to sign tax treaties.

In conclusion, we wish to stress two further points. The first is that the proposals advanced above do not threaten to compromise the personal freedom of Latin investors, but only to promote fairness by bringing their earnings within the tax net. A resident of a country without a tax treaty would have the option of paying withholding tax and retaining anonymity. A resident of a country that does have a tax treaty would not have that option (assuming his home country bases its taxation on the residence principle), but tax treaties include clauses ensuring that information supplied can be used only by the tax authorities and is not transferable to other government agencies, notably the exchange-control authorities. Any violation of this undertaking could result in suspension of the tax treaty. Indeed, it would seem appropriate to maintain tax treaty relationships only with countries whose governments have a record of respecting civil rights—a group now much larger than a few years ago, as a result of the trend toward democracy in many debtor countries. And, of course, anyone who genuinely fears political persecution always has the option of holding assets that do not generate interest income. Thus, our proposals should be exempt from charges that they could facilitate political persecution such as are directed at proposals for indiscriminate disclosure of asset ownership to the governments of source countries.

The second point worth emphasizing is that reversing the erosion of the global fiscal commons is very much in the interest of the major industrial countries as well as developing countries that have suffered capital flight. Their acceptance of this assessment is evidenced by the efforts currently under way within the OECD to negotiate a treaty providing for mutual exchange of information among tax authorities with a view to curbing tax evasion (the Draft Convention on Mutual Administrative Assistance in Tax Matters). The OECD countries owe it to the Third World to make available to them the same opportunities that they are providing among themselves: one wonders whether they should not open this treaty to developing countries.

Deposit Seeking by Banks

Many of the major commercial banks have a second relationship to the debtor countries besides that of creditor to their governments: namely, they have accepted substantial deposits from their citizens. At the same time that their research departments and public spokesmen have been explaining that they can hardly be expected to lend more while the citizens of the debtor countries are showing their lack of confidence by moving money out, the private banking departments of some of those same banks have been actively wooing the fleeing dollars. The pioneering article of Glynn and Koenig (1984) on capital flight recounted the recollection of one rueful New York banker:

When I saw my colleagues in the private banking division at the airport and they said they were making a lot of money. . . I knew the countries the money was coming from were in trouble. When people "vote" with their cash that way, you know the end is nigh. . .

Before condemning the role of the banks in welcoming deposits of flight capital, one should contemplate the defense offered by one thoughtful banker. Schwietert (ch. 8) points out that Swiss secrecy laws were initially designed to protect Jewish depositors moving their assets out of Nazi Germany. Switzerland does not provide secrecy for criminals, or at least for crimes that are recognized as such in Switzerland (which include tax fraud but not tax evasion or the violation of exchange controls). A bank decision to reveal deposits of private citizens to suit the convenience of their governments would represent a massive extension of the coercive power of the state.

These arguments surely deserve respect, even if the Swiss concept of illegality will strike some as restrictive. Yet these arguments do not excuse the provision of "pouch services" to move money out of a country illegally, or the deliberate solicitation of new clients (activities that are indeed already prohibited by the banks' own code of conduct). It is one thing to accept the deposit of a rich foreigner on the same basis as of a poor native. It is quite another to seek private profit by encouraging practices that impoverish the bulk of the population in the source countries. Such activities are no more ethical than the corruption that sometimes provides the source of flight capital. The commercial banks have a responsibility to show decent restraint, and abandon the excuse that some other bank will inevitably do it even if they do not, as their contribution to resolution of the problem of capital flight. One advantage of imposing exchange control, incidentally, is that it prevents the banks from claiming that solicitation of flight capital involves no illegal act and that they are merely matching their competitors.

World Interest Rates

Cuddington (ch. 4) produced statistical support for the proposition that high world interest rates helped to suck funds out of the debtor countries. This provides yet another reason, in addition to the help that lower interest rates would give to the fiscal position in virtually all countries, the stimulus they would give to investment, and the balance of payments relief they would give directly to the debtor countries, for desiring lower real interest rates in the major industrial countries.

To recognize that high international interest rates intensified the exit of capital from debtor countries is to acknowledge that the industrial countries contributed to the problem of resident capital outflow. They need to play their part in ending the problem. A contribution they should make is to reduce real interest rates to historically normal levels.

No one should want to see central banks return to a policy of trying to push interest rates down regardless of the consequences. If markets react to a cut in short-term rates by marking bond prices down, prudence dictates that the effort to reduce rates be called off for the time being. Nonetheless, over time, central banks do have some power to lead interest rates down. Given the current state of the world economy, they should be aiming to use that power unless very strong special circumstances dictate otherwise (for example, a country with an undervalued exchange rate may be justified in maintaining relatively high interest rates to defend its currency). They should most certainly not resist market pressures to lower interest rates in strong-currency countries.

7 Capital Repatriation: Caboose or Locomotive?

Morgan Guaranty (1986) has argued:

LDC capital outflows have to be tackled as part of the solution to the debt problem, not as something that need be addressed only later. If capital flight is given a free ride in the caboose of the LDC debt train, the train has little hope of making the station. It is both necessary and feasible to deal forthrightly with issues affecting capital flight. It is necessary for quantitative and psychological reasons; it is feasible because the causes of capital flight are fairly well understood, and the means exist to stem and reverse it.

Rimmer de Vries repeats this position in chapter 8. He criticizes Dornbusch for stating that the return of flight capital is like the last car of the train, and asserts that he wants to put the caboose up front.

Is it possible to make the repatriation of flight capital the locomotive that would pull the debtor countries out of the debt crisis? The causes do indeed seem reasonably clear, even if econometric problems (notably the limited number of observations) have prevented them from being established as definitively as one would wish. But the policy recommendations to which we have been led—the restoration and maintenance of responsible macroeconomic policies, far-reaching reforms of domestic financial systems, and a switch from the origin to the residence principle of taxation coupled with major efforts to improve tax enforcement involving a willingness to sign tax treaties—are quite demanding, even without adding the restoration of social cohesion and the elimination of corruption. Yet doubt must remain as to whether even the most determined action to "put the house in order" will always guarantee prompt and substantial repatriation of the capital already held abroad, rather than simply prevent further capital flight.

The principal reason for questioning whether capital will return as soon as the reasons that initially caused it to flee have been remedied is the fear that repatriation will expose the investor to penalties for taxes that were unpaid or exchange control regulations that were violated. This fear will be less in countries that lacked exchange controls when the capital fled and which do not attempt to tax investment income earned abroad. This may explain why Argentina and Mexico were the first countries to experience a substantial reflux of flight capital. But, even then, the holders of flight capital may fear that they will be viewed as having unfairly benefited from financial chaos or as having avoided their "fair share" of the adjustment borne by their compatriots. Such perceptions may create political pressures for after-the-fact settlements. This is especially true if the source-country government has been forced to bail out banks or enterprises controlled by individuals or groups with substantial foreign-asset holdings in the wake of withdrawals of funds or borrowings by these individuals.

History abounds with such cases. Kindleberger (ch. 2) chronicles the problems of speculators who profited from the Mississippi bubble in 1718–20:

Keeping profits in notes was risky because they were depreciating, and even buying real property in France—though many including John Law did—was dangerous since most financial troubles in France, and ends of reigns, had been followed by

Chambres de Justice in which excess profits—what we would perhaps call today "undue enrichment"—were examined and fined or confiscated.

Suggestions for similar ex post settlements have been aired in the press of some of the debtor countries in recent years. Glynn and Koenig (1984) documented the concern of the Venezuelan authorities that those with dollar assets should not profit from cheap foreign exchange to service their dollar debts:

In Venezuela, for example—where capital flight was a national pastime until the government finally threw in the towel and devalued the bolivar—a government agency, Recadi, reviews all requests for low-cost dollars. Applicants must first pass through the "department of rejections," where Recadi attempts to uncover hidden dollar assets in subsidiaries or related firms. "A lot of people have tried to get us to pay for their condos in Miami," says Recadi's director, Francisco Maldonado.[29]

These factors create a significant threshold that must be overcome in order to induce the repatriation of funds held abroad. This threshold may be greater than that required to attract funds from nonresidents, despite the relative lack of information and expertise of the latter regarding source-country prospects as well as their greater difficulty in becoming directly involved (due to cultural, social, and linguistic differences as well as explicit barriers to direct foreign investment). It may, in other words, be simpler to live with offshore intermediation than to attract funds back.

What Can Countries Do?

The challenge of recovering flight capital is not a new one, nor is it limited to developing countries. Numerous programs have been proposed and many have been tried. Programs currently in place include France's amnesty with regard to exchange-control violations for residents who repatriate funds held abroad, Chile's debt-for-equity swap program that includes special provisions for residents (ch. 7), which has to date resulted in a reflow of nearly $1 billion, some 5 percent of Chile's debt; and Colombia's "repatriation bonds" (also described in ch. 7). Mexico, in contrast, reports a significant reflow of capital with no program aimed explicitly at recovering flight capital—it has

---

29. Miguel Rodriguez comments that a lot succeeded.

tightened credit to the point where real interest rates rose enormously and simultaneously created major private-sector investment opportunities by realigning its exchange rate and commercial policy.

In general, these programs involve one or more of the following elements:

- an amnesty with regard to past taxes and sanctions for the violation of exchange controls
- favored exchange rates in purchasing domestic assets
- special guarantees against particular fiscal risks.

Each of these has its benefits and costs. One possible cost is the crowding out of new private investment unless the entrepreneur has flight capital at his disposal! It is not clear that this is a desirable basis for selecting new investments.

Amnesty programs, if credible, overcome the "threshold" problem, but they also undercut national authority and may create expectations that tax or other regulations can be violated with impunity in future. Therefore, the decision as to whether to employ an amnesty involves a trade-off between the benefits associated with the recapture of funds and the costs of reduced future enforceability of tax and exchange rate rules.

Favored exchange rates involve transfers to residents holding funds abroad. Thus, they implicitly reward capital flight and tax the capital and immobile factors that remained behind. This too can lead to undesirable and unsustainable expectations over time, increasing the potential danger that residents' financial holdings will become "hot money" in periods of crisis. In extreme cases, the creation of an arbitrage potential between rates of return available to residents with funds outside the country and those with only domestic assets will lead to "round tripping" where capital will flow out in order to take advantage of the inward arbitrage. This is a primary concern in the design and management of debt-for-equity swap programs (Zedillo, ch. 7). If such programs are perceived as inequitable, they will undermine the legitimacy of government policy.

In those cases where residents with foreign holdings place a high value on preserving their anonymity to avoid economic or political reprisals, credibility is even more difficult to obtain. So called whitener bonds, bearer bonds sold offshore that can be converted for domestic use, have been employed in some cases. A limitation of these schemes is that the anonymity is retained only as long as residents are content to invest locally on a passive, arms-length basis. One can add the option of converting to local currency to permit holders to invest in directly controlled operations, but anonymity inevitably ends when that option is exercised.

Special guarantees, such as allowing dollar-denominated bank accounts for residents bringing foreign exchange or guaranteeing the convertibility of "registered" inflows will, if credible, reduce the fiscal risks faced. However, such special treatment of returning resident capital implicitly subordinates other domestic claims, increasing their exposure to risk. Thus, they could exacerbate "arbitrage" capital flight in periods of crisis. Further, given the track record of many countries with respect to such guarantees, for example, Mexico's treatment of Mex-dollar accounts, it is unlikely that they will be fully credible, especially in cases where there is a large overhang of external sovereign debt with even more senior status.

Offshore Intermediation

In his survey of history, Kindleberger (ch. 2) pointed out that Argentines were important buyers of Argentine bonds floated on the London capital market in the late nineteenth century. Similarly, India has recently created a mutual fund to allow Indian expatriates to invest in Indian industry, Mexicans are known to be significant purchasers of Mexican securities in US markets, and Latin businessmen are understood to borrow from Miami banks using their deposits in the same banks as collateral.[30]

The existence of such offshore intermediation casts doubt on the proposition that foreign placement of funds can be explained in terms of portfolio diversification, since most of the risks to which the investor chooses to expose himself are those of his domestic economy. Indeed, the fact that the investor chooses to expose himself to those risks despite having taken his funds abroad suggests that he feels more comfortable with the economic risks of the economy that he knows. What he must be seeking is either a more liquid medium (perhaps assuring convertibility into foreign exchange) for his assets than offered by local markets, the chance to change the currency

---

30. The advantages of this procedure are that, in his capacity as foreign borrower, the businessman gets access to official exchange to service his debt while, if things go wrong at home, he would retain a foreign asset provided that he could get the debt taken off his hands when he sold the company.

denomination of his claim so as to evade the risk of devaluation of the local currency, the opportunity of evading taxation, or else protection through anonymity and the leverage provided by the foreign jurisdiction vis-à-vis those country risks that weigh more heavily on resident than on nonresident capital.

With regard to anonymity, offshore intermediation can provide an effective laundering of funds to reduce the risk of ex post claims or sanctions. Further, it provides residents with nonresident bedfellows which may provide some protection against attempts to impose reprisals.

To the extent that offshore intermediation can be relied on to recycle funds back to the local economy, capital flight would not have some of the damaging effects analyzed above ("Consequences"). In particular, it would not aggravate the foreign-exchange or savings shortage. It would still, of course, impede the development of local financial markets. If it involves acquisition of a claim denominated in foreign exchange, it would increase the social cost of devaluation. And it would still leave the perverse redistribution of income and wealth and attendant fiscal problem.

The main problem with offshore intermediation, however, would appear to be that it is not a reliable form of recycling. Domestic residents may be willing to recycle their funds, or some part of their funds, under normal circumstances, but the moments of acute national emergency, when the need to conserve foreign exchange is greatest, are precisely those when newly fleeing money is least likely to be recycled and previously recycled money is most likely to flee. Thus, in most cases, offshore intermediation would not seem an attractive long-run solution. Its most useful role may be as a first stage in the return of flight capital.

Should Countries Seek to Recapture Flight Capital?

While one might be tempted to take it as axiomatic that countries should seek to recapture flight capital, the issue is at what cost and to what end. How much better terms should a country be willing to offer residents with funds abroad than those without or than nonresidents? What special benefits will such recapture bring? While it will improve the image of a source country in world financial circles, there is no assurance that this would lead to more favorable terms on outstanding debt. Further, there is no reason to expect recaptured funds to be less footloose in case of future crises than either foreign funds or new resident savings. However, to the extent that such funds are more likely to be combined effectively with local management and entrepreneurship, they might be considerably more valuable than inflows of foreign capital.

Some countries may find it impossible to translate policy reforms into renewed growth without an initial injection of foreign exchange provided by the repatriation of flight capital. The obverse problem is that the amnesties necessary to secure a rapid repatriation of capital may undermine the rule of law and hence respect for the policy reforms. It does not seem possible to offer a general conclusion as to which of these dangers is greatest, but two criteria are highly relevant:

- the magnitude of the sums currently held abroad by residents relative to the alternative sources of foreign exchange available to the country

- the feasibility of convincing the public that any amnesty is once-and-for-all.

Countries with relatively adequate foreign exchange availability are probably well-advised to learn to live with offshore intermediation until funds seep back of their own accord. But countries that have suffered massive outflows and have little alternative prospect of restoring growth should examine whether they cannot make a credible commitment to a once-and-for-all amnesty. The worst of all worlds would be to allow policy to be paralyzed between these two solutions.

8 Summary and Conclusions

We defined capital flight as resident capital that flees from the perception of abnormal risks at home. We argued, however, that a more interesting concept to measure than capital flight was *total* outflows of resident capital, including "normal" portfolio diversification, because a loss of domestic savings to a savings-short economy has the same ill consequences whether or not it is "normal." In practice, of course, resident capital outflow is a serious problem only when normal outflows are reinforced by capital flight.

Our concern with outflows of capital from developing countries is not a rejection of the desirability of international integration of financial markets. Rather it reflects the view that poor countries can and should be able to retain their domestic savings at home, as well as draw on foreign savings. Ideally this might be achieved with domestic holding of foreign assets for security and diversification purposes being offset by foreign holdings of (risky) domestic assets, but in the absence of suitable offsetting investments it is necessary to be concerned if outward flows become sizable.

Despite the effort that has recently been invested in estimating resident capital outflow, there remains a great margin of uncertainty about the statistics. It is nevertheless clear that a great deal of money—probably approaching $100 billion from just five of the principal countries involved (Argentina, Brazil, Mexico, the Philippines, and Venezuela)—did flee. Argentina, Mexico, and Venezuela were particularly heavily affected. Significant sums have started to return to some countries in the past 18 months or so.

Two general theories have been advanced to explain capital flight. One points to a deficient overall investment climate resulting from macroeconomic mismanagement that raises fears of currency devaluation, inflation, fiscal deficits, low growth, and a debt overhang. The other focuses on discriminatory treatment of resident capital in the form of taxes, financial repression, and the nonavailability of foreign-exchange denomination of claims, and subordination to nonresident claims in the event of financial crisis. Unlike the overall investment-climate theory, the discriminatory-treatment theory can explain resident capital outflows that coincide with nonresident inflows. It is therefore the natural explanation for the capital flight that antedated the debt crisis. Conversely, the discriminatory-treatment theory cannot explain the persistence of resident capital outflows after voluntary lending to the debtor countries dried up in 1982: the natural explanation is inadequacy of the overall investment climate. Empirical studies seem to point particularly clearly to the role of currency overvaluation. Presumably the recent repatriation of capital to Argentina and Mexico reflects some improvement in the investment climate as well as high real interest rates.

Resident capital outflow is generally bad for the country involved and bad for the world as a whole. This is not to deny that it results from rational and perfectly understandable behavior on the part of wealth-owners, nor indeed that it may at times serve to induce desirable policy changes. Nevertheless, resident capital outflow from a country that is a natural net capital importer necessarily implies either that investment, and therefore growth, is lower than it need be, or that the country is a bigger gross borrower from the world capital market, with the attendant financial exposure. In the former case, a loss of domestic capital may intensify the foreign-exchange constraint as well as the savings constraint, and thus dictate a cutback in current output as well as future growth. In either case, resident capital outflow means the exportation of financial intermediation and therefore stultification of the growth of domestic financial markets. It may also lead to a fiscal crisis, and hence inflation, and a massive perverse redistribution of income and wealth. In the worst case, domestic capitalists may start looking for more challenging foreign investment opportunities than liquid assets and real estate, leading their native societies to lose not just their capital but also their entrepreneurial energies and their economic stake in national policies.

The primary responsibility for stemming resident capital outflows rests on the source countries, for it is their inadequate policies that turned the minor problem of normal outflow into the major problem of capital flight. Our four key policy recommendations may be summarized as follows:

● restoration and maintenance of responsible macroeconomic policies involving competitive exchange rates, positive but nonprohibitive real interest rates, and fiscal probity, hopefully leading to the restoration of economic growth

● reform of the domestic financial system to make it less dependent on government intervention and more resilient to shocks

● a pragmatic attitude to exchange controls that avoids regarding them as a substitute for sound policies and recognizes that they cannot attract back money that has already fled, while using them in appropriate circumstances to limit the exodus of new savings

● a decision to base the tax system on the residence principle and a major effort to improve tax enforcement, involving in particular a willingness to sign tax treaties so as to secure an exchange of information with the principal haven countries that will permit the collection of taxes due on foreign investment income.

Capital outflows from debtor countries are also importantly influenced by policies in the haven countries, however, as the significant coefficient on US interest rates in some estimates of the causes of resident capital outflows has confirmed. The haven countries have a duty to help resolve this problem, in the following ways:

- by imposing a substantial withholding tax on all nonresident investment income, which would be refundable on evidence that the recipient had reported the income to his national tax authority, coupled with a continued or an enhanced willingness to sign tax treaties so as to enable the source countries to tax the foreign investment income of their residents

- by the private banking departments of commercial banks ending the deliberate solicitation of new clients in developing countries and the provision of "pouch services"

- by continuing efforts to reduce real interest rates to historically normal levels.

The most important priority is to stop the hemorrhage of new capital outflow rather than to attract back the money that has already fled. Whether special efforts (tax amnesties or "whitener bonds") are worth making to attract capital back depends on the size of the stock held abroad and the possibilities of securing adequate finance from other sources, and also the feasibility of carrying credibility with a commitment that these are once-and-for-all measures.

Although some capital returned to two of the three principal source countries in the past 18 months, it would be wrong to think that the problem of capital flight has already been resolved. The price of that repatriation has been extremely high interest rates—far higher than are consistent with an investment boom and hence the restoration of growth prospects. Moreover, recent reports indicate renewed capital flight from Argentina. While much progress has been made toward the institution of responsible macroeconomic policies and several countries are getting to grips with needed reforms of their domestic financial systems, there has as yet been no action on the needed fiscal reforms. Moreover, resolution of the problem will require confidence that these changes will be maintained over the long haul and not allowed to slip once the money returns. The challenge remains, in Kindleberger's words, "quite an order."

References

Balassa, Bela, Gerardo M. Bueno, Pedro-Pablo Kuczynski, and Mario Henrique Simonsen. 1986. *Toward Renewed Economic Growth in Latin America.* Mexico City: El Colegio de Mexico; Rio de Janeiro: Fundaçao Getúlio Vargas; Washington: Institute for International Economics.

Conesa, Eduardo R. 1987. *The Causes of Capital Flight from Latin America.* Washington: Inter-American Development Bank.

Cuddington, John T. 1986. *Capital Flight: Estimates, Issues, and Explanations,* Princeton Studies in International Finance, no. 58. Princeton, NJ:International Finance Section, Department of Economics, Princeton University.

Deppler, Michael, and Martin Williamson. 1987. "Capital Flight: Concepts, Measurement, and Issues." In *Staff Studies for the World Economic Outlook.* Washington: International Monetary Fund, August, pp. 39–58.

Diaz Alejandro, Carlos. 1984. "Latin American Debt: I Don't Think We Are in Kansas Anymore." *Brookings Papers on Economic Activity,* no. 2.

Dooley, Michael, William Helkie, Ralph Tryon and John Underwood. 1986. "An Analysis of External Debt Positions of Eight Developing Countries Through 1990." *Journal of Development Economics,* vol. 21, no 2, pp. 283–318.

Dooley, Michael. 1986. "Country-Specific Risk Premiums, Capital Flight and Net Investment Income Payments in Selected Developing Countries," DM 86/17. Washington: International Monetary Fund.

Dornbusch, Rudiger. 1985. "External Debt, Budget Deficits and Disequilibrium Exchange Rates." In *International Debt and the Developing Countries,* edited by Gordon W. Smith and John T. Cuddington. Washington: World Bank.

Eaton, Jonathan. 1987. "Public Debt Guarantees and Private Capital Flight." *World Bank Economic Review,* vol. 1, no. 3 (May), pp. 377–95.

Eaton, Jonathan; Mark Gersovitz; and Joseph E. Stiglitz. 1986. "The Pure Theory of Country Risk." *European Economic Review,* vol. 4, no. 30, pp. 481–513.

Erbe, Susanne. 1985. "The Flight of Capital from Developing Countries." *Intereconomics,* (November/December).

Frieden, Jeff. 1981. "Third World Indebted Industrialization: International Finance and State Capitalism in Mexico, Brazil, Algeria, and South Korea." *International Organization,* vol. 35, no. 3, pp. 407–32.

Gennotte, Gerard; Homi Kharas; and Sayeed Sadeq 1987. "A Valuation Model for LDC Debt with Endogenous Reschedulings." *World Bank Economic Review,* vol. 1, no. 2, pp. 237–72.

Gillis, Malcolm; Donald Lessard; and Glenn Jenkins. 1982. "Public Enterprise Finance: Toward a Synthesis." In *Public Enterprise in Less Developed Countries,* edited by Leroy P. Jones et al. Cambridge: Cambridge University Press.

Glynn, Lenny, and Peter Koenig. 1984. "The Capital Flight Crisis." *Institutional Investor,* international edition. (November), pp. 109–19.

Guzman Calafell, Javier, and Jesus Alvarez Gutierrez. 1987. *Las Fugas de Capital en Mexico: Un Analisis Critico de los Planteamientos Recientes.* Mexico City: Banco de Mexico.

Ize, Alain, and Guillermo Ortiz. 1987. "Fiscal Rigidities, Public Debt, and Capital Flight," IMF *Staff Papers*, vol. 34, no. 2 (June), pp. 311–33.
Khan, Mohsin S., and Nadeem Ul Haque. 1985. "Foreign Borrowing and Capital Flight: A Formal Analysis." IMF *Staff Papers*, vol. 32, no. 4 (December), pp. 606–28.
———. 1987. "Capital Flight from Developing Countries," *Finance and Development* (March).
Kindleberger, Charles P. 1937. *International Short-Term Capital Movements*. New York, NY: Augustus Kelley.
Kraft, Joseph. 1984. *The Mexican Rescue*. New York, NY: Group of Thirty.
Lessard, Donald R. 1987. "Country Risk and the Structure of International Financial Intermediation." Federal Reserve Bank of Conference on Financial Risk, St. Louis, Mo., forthcoming.
Lessard, Donald R., and John Williamson. 1987. *Capital Flight and Third World Debt*. Washington: Institute for International Economics.
Magee, Stephen P., and William A. Brock. 1986. "Third World Debt and International Capital Market Failure as a Consequence of Redistributive Political Risk Sharing." In *World Debt Crisis: International Lending on Trial*, edited by Michael P. Claudon. Cambridge, Mass.: Ballinger.
Merton, Robert C. 1977. "An Analytic Derivation of the Cost of Loan Guarantees and Deposit Insurance: An Application of Modern Option Pricing Theory." *Journal of Banking and Finance*, no. 1, pp 3–11.
Morgan Guaranty. 1986. "LDC Capital Flight." *World Financial Markets* (March).
——— 1987. "LDC Debt Realities," *World Financial Markets* (June–July).
Protopapadakis, Aris. 1985. "An Analysis of Government Credit 'Crises.'" Federal Reserve Bank of Philadelphia, Working Paper, no. 85–14.
Tobin, James. 1977. "How Dead is Keynes?" *Economic Inquiry* (October).
Williamson, John. 1983. *The Open Economy and the World Economy*. New York, NY: Basic Books.
World Bank. 1985. *World Development Report—1985*. Washington.

Appendix

Participants, Conference on Capital Flight, Institute for International Economics, Washington, October 2–4, 1986

Osvaldo R. Agatiello
Banco Central de la Republica Argentina
Buenos Aires

James E. Ammerman
Department of the Treasury
Washington

Dragoslav Avramovíc
Bank of Credit and Commerce International
Washington

George B. N. Ayittey
Bloomsburg University
Bloomsburg, Pa.

Norman A. Bailey
Colby, Bailey and Associates
Washington

Bela Balassa
Institute for International Economics
Washington

C. Fred Bergsten
Institute for International Economics
Washington

Jagdish Bhagwati
World Bank
Washington

David R. Bock
World Bank
Washington

David E. Bodner
Bank Julius Baer
New York, NY

Eduardo R. Conesa
Inter-American Development Bank
Washington

Hugh W. Conway
Federal Deposit Insurance Corporation
Washington

Vittorio Corbo
World Bank
Washington

John T. Cuddington
Georgetown University
Washington

Robert E. Cumby
New York University
New York, NY

Jorge Daly
AFL-CIO
Washington

David T. Devlin
Citibank
New York, NY

Robert Devlin
United Nations Economic Commission
  for Latin America and the Caribbean
Santiago

José A. Diaz-Asper
ATC Consortium
Washington

Michael P. Dooley
International Monetary Fund
Washington

Rudiger Dornbusch
Massachusetts Institute of Technology
Cambridge, Mass.

Vance van Dyne
Morgan Stanley International
New York, NY

Jorge Espinosa-Carranza
Inter-American Development Bank
Washington

Thomas L. Farmer
Prather, Seeger, Doolittle & Farmer
Washington

Richard E. Feinberg
Overseas Development Council
Washington

Ava S. Feiner
IBM
Washington

C. David Finch
International Monetary Fund
Washington

Isaiah Frank
Johns Hopkins University
Washington

Erhard Fürst
Creditanstalt
Vienna

Sunil Gulati
Columbia University
New York, NY

José Angel Gurria
Ministry of Finance
Mexico City

Efraim Gutkino
Trade Development Bank
Geneva, Switzerland

Carleton R. Haswell
Chemical Bank
New York, NY

H. Robert Heller
Federal Reserve Board
Washington

C. Randall Henning
Institute for International Economics
Washington

Richard J. Herring
University of Pennsylvania
Philadelphia, Pa.

James S. Henry
New York, NY

Rudolf Hommes
Estrategia Económica
Bogotá

William C. Hood
International Monetary Fund
Washington

Shafiqul Islam
Institute for International Economics
Washington

Alain Ize
International Monetary Fund
Washington

Fred Z. Jaspersen
World Bank
Washington

Alexandre Kafka
International Monetary Fund
Washington

Suhas L. Ketkar
Marine Midland Bank
New York, NY

G. Russell Kincaid
International Monetary Fund
Washington

Charles P. Kindleberger
Massachusetts Institute of Technology
Cambridge, Mass.

Linda P. Kinney
Department of State
Washington

Norman R. Klath
Morgan Guaranty Trust Company
New York, NY

Charles Kovacs
Chase Manhattan Bank
New York, NY

Pedro-Pablo Kuczynski
First Boston International
New York, NY

Donald R. Lessard
Massachusetts Institute of Technology
Cambridge, Mass.

Richard M. Levich
New York University
New York, NY

Frank E. Loy
German Marshall Fund
Washington

Richard T. McCormack
Organization of American States
Washington

William J. McFadden
Department of the Treasury
Washington

Carlos A. Massad
United Nations Economic Commission
  for Latin America and the Caribbean and
  University of Santiago
Santiago

Hyman P. Minsky
Washington University
St. Louis, Mo.

Jeremiah L. Murphy
Siemens Capital Corporation
Washington

Marcus Noland
Institute for International Economics
Washington

Richard R. O'Brien
American Express Bank
London

Barbara N. Opper
World Bank
Washington

Carlos Paredes
Brookings Institution
Washington

Guy Pierre Pfeffermann
World Bank
Washington

Jorge Pinto
Embassy of Mexico
Washington

Rafael Pozas
Embassy of Mexico
Washington

Peter J. Quirk
International Monetary Fund
Washington

Joseph R. Ramos
United Nations Economic Commission for
  Latin America and the Caribbean
Santiago

John G. Rehak
Siemens Capital Corporation
Washington

Alfred Reifman
Congressional Research Service
Washington

Eli M. Remolona
Federal Reserve Bank of New York

Wolfgang Rieke
Deutsche Bundesbank
Frankfurt, Germany

Rhys Robinson
Institute for International Economics
Washington

Miguel Rodriguez F.
Instituto de Estudios Superiores de Administración
Caracas

Riordan Roett
Johns Hopkins University
Washington

John B. Ross
Institute of International Finance
Washington

Robert Samuelson
Newsweek
Washington

Horst Schulman
Institute of International Finance
Washington

Aloys Schwietert
Swiss Bank Corporation
Basel, Switzerland

Michael R. Sesit
Wall Street Journal
New York, NY

Barbara B. Stallings
University of Wisconsin
Madison, Wis.

Leon S. Tarrant
Comptroller of the Currency
Washington

Jane L. Barber Thery
Institute for International Economics
Washington

Edwin M. Truman
Federal Reserve Board
Washington

Miguel Urrutia
Inter-American Development Bank
Washington

Philip K. Verleger Jr.
Institute for International Economics
Washington

Rimmer de Vries
Morgan Guaranty Trust
New York, NY

Ingo Walter
New York University
New York, NY

Richard G. Ware
Bank of England
London

Alfred J. Watkins
Joint Economic Committee
Washington

Richard C. Webb
Universidad Católica
Lima

Peter J. West
Institute of International Finance
Washington

Howard Wiarda
American Enterprise Institute
Washington

John Williamson
Institute for International Economics
Washington

Martin C. Williamson
International Monetary Fund
Washington

Paul Wonnacott
Institute for International Economics
Washington

Ernesto Zedillo
Banco de Mexico
Mexico City

Other Publications from the Institute

POLICY ANALYSES IN INTERNATIONAL ECONOMICS SERIES

1 **The Lending Policies of the International Monetary Fund**
   John Williamson/August 1982

2 **"Reciprocity": A New Approach to World Trade Policy?**
   William R. Cline/September 1982

3 **Trade Policy in the 1980s**
   C. Fred Bergsten and William R. Cline/November 1982

4 **International Debt and the Stability of the World Economy**
   William R. Cline/September 1983

5 **The Exchange Rate System, Second Edition**
   John Williamson/September 1983, rev. June 1985

6 **Economic Sanctions in Support of Foreign Policy Goals**
   Gary Clyde Hufbauer and Jeffrey J. Schott/October 1983

7 **A New SDR Allocation?**
   John Williamson/March 1984

8 **An International Standard for Monetary Stabilization**
   Ronald I. McKinnon/March 1984

9 **The Yen/Dollar Agreement: Liberalizing Japanese Capital Markets**
   Jeffrey A. Frankel/December 1984

10 **Bank Lending to Developing Countries: The Policy Alternatives**
   C. Fred Bergsten, William R. Cline, and John Williamson/April 1985

11 **Trading for Growth: The Next Round of Trade Negotiations**
   Gary Clyde Hufbauer and Jeffrey J. Schott/September 1985

12 **Financial Intermediation Beyond the Debt Crisis**
   Donald R. Lessard and John Williamson/September 1985

13 **The United States–Japan Economic Problem**
   C. Fred Bergsten and William R. Cline/October 1985, rev. January 1987

14 **Deficits and the Dollar: The World Economy at Risk**
   Stephen Marris/December 1985

15 **Trade Policy for Troubled Industries**
   Gary Clyde Hufbauer and Howard F. Rosen/March 1986

16 **The United States and Canada: The Quest for Free Trade**
   Paul Wonnacott, with an Appendix by John Williamson/March 1987

17 **Adjusting to Success: Balance of Payments Policy in the East Asian NICs**
   Bela Balassa and John Williamson/June 1987

18 Mobilizing Bank Lending to Debtor Countries
    William R. Cline/June 1987

19 Auction Quotas and United States Trade Policy
    C. Fred Bergsten, Kimberly Ann Elliott, Jeffrey J. Schott, and Wendy E. Takacs/September 1987

20 Agriculture and the GATT: Rewriting the Rules
    Dale E. Hathaway/September 1987

21 Anti-Protection: Changing Forces in United States Trade Politics
    I. M. Destler and John S. Odell/September 1987

22 Targets and Indicators: A Blueprint for the International Coordination of Economic Policy
    John Williamson and Marcus H. Miller/September 1987

BOOKS

IMF Conditionality
John Williamson, editor/1983

Trade Policy in the 1980s
William R. Cline, editor/1983

Subsidies in International Trade
Gary Clyde Hufbauer and Joanna Shelton Erb/1984

International Debt: Systemic Risk and Policy Response
William R. Cline/1984

Economic Sanctions Reconsidered: History and Current Policy
Gary Clyde Hufbauer and Jeffrey J. Schott, assisted by Kimberly Ann Elliott/1985

Trade Protection in the United States: 31 Case Studies
Gary Clyde Hufbauer, Diane T. Berliner, and Kimberly Ann Elliott/1986

Toward Renewed Economic Growth in Latin America
Bela Balassa, Gerardo M. Bueno, Pedro-Pablo Kuczynski, and Mario Henrique Simonsen/1986

American Trade Politics: System Under Stress
I.M. Destler/1986

The Future of World Trade in Textiles and Apparel
William R. Cline/1987

Capital Flight and Third World Debt
Donald R. Lessard and John Williamson, editors/1987

SPECIAL REPORTS

1 **Promoting World Recovery: A Statement on Global Economic Strategy**
   by Twenty-six Economists from Fourteen Countries/December 1982

2 **Prospects for Adjustment in Argentina, Brazil, and Mexico: Responding to the Debt Crisis**
   John Williamson, editor/June 1983

3 **Inflation and Indexation: Argentina, Brazil, and Israel**
   John Williamson, editor/March 1985

4 **Global Economic Imbalances**
   C. Fred Bergsten, editor/March 1986

5 **African Debt and Financing**
   Carol Lancaster and John Williamson, editors/May 1986

FORTHCOMING

The United States as a Debtor Country
C. Fred Bergsten and Shafiqul Islam

Domestic Adjustment and International Trade
Gary Clyde Hufbauer and Howard F. Rosen, editors

Japan in the World Economy
Bela Balassa and Marcus Noland

World Economic Problems
Kimberly Ann Elliott and John Williamson, editors

Correcting the United States Trade Deficit: The Global Impact
William R. Cline and Stephen Marris

Energy Policies for the 1990s: A Global Perspective
Philip K. Verleger, Jr.

The Outlook for World Commodity Prices
Philip K. Verleger, Jr.

POLICY ANALYSES IN INTERNATIONAL ECONOMICS 23

Capital Flight: The Problem and Policy Responses
Donald R. Lessard and John Williamson

This study addresses the problem of capital flight from Third World debtor countries and analyzes policy measures that might stem and reverse the flow. Such outflows are estimated at about $86 billion for the six major debtor countries (Argentina, Brazil, Korea, Mexico, the Philippines, Venezuela) during 1976-84, varying from zero in Korea to $30 billion in Venezuela.

OTHER INSTITUTE PUBLICATIONS

POLICY ANALYSES IN INTERNATIONAL ECONOMICS Series

18   *Mobilizing Bank Lending to Debtor Countries*
William R. Cline
1987   ISBN 0–88132–062–5   100 pp.

12   *Financial Intermediation Beyond the Debt Crisis*
Donald R. Lessard and John Williamson
1985   ISBN 0–88132–021–8   130 pp.

10   *Bank Lending to Developing Countries: The Policy Alternatives*
C. Fred Bergsten, William R. Cline, and John Williamson
1985 ISBN 0-88132-032-3 221 pp.

BOOKS

Capital Flight and Third World Debt
Donald R. Lessard and John Williamson, editors
1987   ISBN 0-88132-053-6   c.240 pp.

Toward Renewed Economic Growth in Latin America
Bela Balassa, Gerardo M. Bueno, Pedro-Pablo Kuczynski, and Mario Henrique Simonsen
1986   ISBN 0–88132–045–5   205 pp.

International Debt: Systemic Risk and Policy Response
William R. Cline
1984   ISBN 0-88132-015-3   336 pp.

SPECIAL REPORTS

5   *African Debt and Financing*
Carol Lancaster and John Williamson, editors
1986   ISBN 0–88132–044–7   229 pp.

Institute for International Economics
11 Dupont Circle, NW, Washington, DC 20036   ISBN 0–88132–059–5